2.⁵⁰

North Carolina Lighthouses

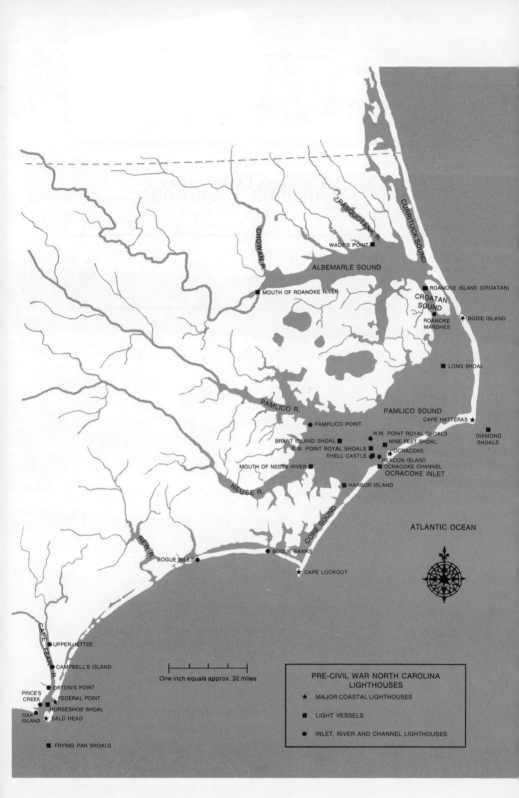

CHOWAN R.

PASQUOTANK R.

CURRITUCK SOUND

WADE'S POINT

ALBEMARLE SOUND

MOUTH OF ROANOKE RIVER

ROANOKE ISLAND (CROATAN)

CROATAN SOUND

ROANOKE MARSHES

BODIE ISLAND

LONG SHOAL

PAMLICO R.

PAMLICO SOUND

CAPE HATTERAS

PAMPLICO POINT

DIAMOND SHOALS

N.W. POINT ROYAL SHOALS

BRANT ISLAND SHOAL

NINE FEET SHOAL

S.W. POINT ROYAL SHOALS

OCRACOKE

SHELL CASTLE

BEACON ISLAND

MOUTH OF NEUSE RIVER

OCRACOKE CHANNEL

OCRACOKE INLET

NEUSE R.

HARBOR ISLAND

CORE SOUND

ATLANTIC OCEAN

NEW R.

BOGUE INLET

BOGUE BANKS

CAPE LOOKOUT

One inch equals approx. 32 miles

CAPE FEAR R.

UPPER JETTEE

CAMPBELL'S ISLAND

PRICE'S CREEK

ORTON'S POINT

FEDERAL POINT

HORSESHOE SHOAL

OAK ISLAND

BALD HEAD

FRYING PAN SHOALS

PRE-CIVIL WAR NORTH CAROLINA
LIGHTHOUSES

★ MAJOR COASTAL LIGHTHOUSES

■ LIGHT VESSELS

● INLET, RIVER AND CHANNEL LIGHTHOUSES

North Carolina Lighthouses

by

David Stick

Raleigh
North Carolina Department of Cultural Resources
Division of Archives and History
Third Printing, 1982

DEPARTMENT OF CULTURAL RESOURCES
ISBN 0-86526-191-1

SARA W. HODGKINS
Secretary

DIVISION OF ARCHIVES AND HISTORY
WILLIAM S. PRICE, JR.
Director

SUELLEN M. HOY
Assistant Director

Contents

Maps and Illustrations vii
Foreword ix
Introduction xi
1   In the Beginning 1
2   The North Carolina Coast 5
3   The First North Carolina Lighthouses 11
4   Guarding the Coast 18
5   Light Vessels 25
6   Cape Fear River Lights 35
7   Filling in the Blind Spots 42
8   The Light House Board Takes Over 48
9   The Lights Go Out 53
10   Screw-Pile Lighthouses 58
11   Majestic Coastal Towers 63
12   Conclusion 71
A Note on Research Sources 77
Index 79

Maps and Illustrations

Map of pre-Civil War North Carolina Lighthouses ... Frontispiece
Pharos of Alexandria xii
John White Paintings of Indians 3
John White Map of North Carolina Coast, 1585 6
Wimble Map of North Carolina Coast, 1733 8
Entrance of Cape Fear River, 1805 13
Shell Castle Lighthouse 16
Cape Hatteras Lighthouse 20
Ocracoke Light Station 24
Diamond Shoals Lightships 26
Map of Cape Fear River Lights 34
Bald Head Lighthouse 36
Oak Island Light 39
"The Old Lighthouse," Price's Creek 40
Price's Creek Light 41
Cape Lookout Light Station 50
Cape Lookout Lighthouse ...:.............................. 51
Map of War at Hatteras Inlet, 1861 54
Harbor Island Light 59
Roanoke Marshes Light 60
Cape Hatteras Lighthouse 62
Cape Hatteras Light Station 65
Bodie Island Light Station 67
Cape Hatteras, Cape Lookout, Bodie Island Lighthouses 68
Currituck Beach Light Station 69
Map of North Carolina Lighthouses 70
Cape Fear Light 72
Frying Pan Shoals 73
Diamond Shoals 74

Foreword

Because of North Carolina's treacherous coastline, there has been throughout Tar Heel history the need to warn sailors of impending danger as they neared the Outer Banks. The story of efforts to provide needed protection, from colonial days until modern times, is filled with fascination. Lighthouses, and supplemental lightboats, made coastal shipping possible and provided protection to those venturing near the Outer Banks. The history of the construction and operation of lighthouses and vessels is recounted vividly and interestingly in this pamphlet by David Stick.

Mr. Stick, an authority on the Outer Banks, is well known for his books including *Fabulous Dare, Graveyard of the Atlantic, The Outer Banks of North Carolina, 1584-1958*, and *The Cape Hatteras Seashore*. His brief history of Dare County, published as one of the Archives and History series, has been well received; and it is anticipated that his story of lighthouses will be unusually popular and will be enjoyed by anyone having an interest in the sea.

Dr. Jeffrey J. Crow, head of the General Publications Branch, Historical Publications Section, Division of Archives and History, edited the manuscript and assumed responsibility for seeing it through the press. Mrs. Patricia R. Johnson assisted with the proofreading.

Memory F. Mitchell
Historical Publications Administrator

June 20, 1979

Introduction

This is the story of North Carolina's coastal lighthouses: tall, circular structures, graceful yet imposing, towering incongruously above the low-lying sand banks at scattered intervals along our Atlantic shoreline.

It is the story of the men who designed and built and manned them, and of other men whose lives and vessels were saved because they were there. And it is the story of why they were built and how they were built and why these North Carolina coastal lighthouses were projects of the federal government instead of the state.

But it is more!

It is the story of the continuing yet often futile efforts to assure safe passage for mariners along hundreds of miles of narrow channels meandering through the shifting shoals of our inlets and across our broad sounds and up our network of interior rivers. It is the story of pre-Civil War light vessels, riding at anchor in the most exposed locations throughout that vast network of inland waters; and of the ungainly looking structures which replaced them, the screw-pile lighthouses, built out in the water at places with names like Brant Island Shoal and Wade's Point and Roanoke Marshes.

Finally, it is the story of advancing technology: of the progression from whale oil to coal oil to electricity as fuel for the lights; from stakes and barrels marking innumerable lesser channels, to modern automated devices that turn lights on and off and ring bells and horns; and from stubby lightships that could never seem to weather the storms and remain on station off our treacherous capes, to modernistic four-legged Texas tower-like monsters that have been built there to stay.

The Pharos of Alexandria, archaeologists have estimated, rose to a height of 450 feet, from which it would have been visible at a distance of twenty-nine miles. The tower survived for nearly fifteen centuries before being toppled by an earthquake around 1200 A.D. This engraving appeared in John Harris's *Complete Collection of Voyages and Travels* (London, 1744), I, p. 415. (Photo courtesy of the Rare Book Room, Perkins Library, Duke University, Durham, North Carolina.)

In the Beginning

When Englishmen first reached the coast of present-day North Carolina nearly four hundred years ago, they were greeted by native Indians traveling in large log canoes. In the absence of metal tools the Indians made these craft by hollowing out the trunks of trees, first burning holes, and then chipping away with sharp shells to attain the shape and size they wanted. Some of the canoes were large enough to carry several men, and though by our modern standards they would appear clumsy and hard to control, the Indians traveled in them regularly from island to island.

No doubt when Wingina the chief, and Granganimo his brother, and others of their tribe set out in a small flotilla of these crude vessels to travel, say, from the mainland to Roanoke Island they had little difficulty finding their way and steering clear of underwater shoals. For they had been traveling those same routes since childhood, and their ancestors before them; and like aborigine mariners the world over they had long since come to recognize the markings of specific hills and cliffs, tall trees and open areas, and to use these landmarks as aids to navigation.

Sir Walter Raleigh's explorers and colonists, on the other hand, made the ocean-going voyage from England to America in much larger vessels, under sail, in search of new horizons, much as other Europeans had been doing since before the birth of Christ.

When man started building these larger vessels, capable of carrying extensive cargo and seaworthy enough to enable him to travel considerable distances from his home port, it became more and more important to be able to identify prominent headlands and other easily distinguishable features that stood out against the skyline.

Probably the heaviest concentration of early maritime commerce was in the vicinity of the Mediterranean Sea, and the experienced navigator sailing along the coast of Spain toward that vast interior body of water learned to keep an eye open for the Rock of Gibraltar, with full knowledge that it clearly marked the entrance to the Mediterranean.

Undoubtedly the use of light to guide vessels at night began when someone built a bonfire on shore at the entrance to a harbor. Similarly, where there were no unusual natural features to serve as harbor markers in the daytime, someone erected a cross or a tower, or maybe even arranged a pile of rock or stone in a distinctive form.

It probably was not long before some enterprising individual came up with the idea of combining the two, the light to provide guidance at night and the structure to help out in the daylight, building an open fire on top of a pyramid of rocks, for example, thus opening the way for what we now know as lighthouses.

One of the first recorded instances of lighthouse construction was more than two thousand years ago, possibly as early as 300 B.C., when the Egyptians began assembling a massive tower on the little island of Pharos at the entrance to the port of Alexandria. Built of marble and reportedly 450 feet high, with a large open wood fire on top, it was dedicated by the Egyptians "for the safety of mariners." A drawing, published in 1744, long after it was destroyed by an earthquake, shows a huge multistoried structure, larger by far than any lighthouse built in modern times.

The Romans are reported to have built at least thirty lighthouses before the decline of their empire, and one lighthouse built either by them or by the Phoenicians some two thousand years ago is still in use. This is the famed Tower of Hercules on the northwest coast of Spain, originally constructed of square stone to a height of 130 feet, with an open fire on top that reputedly burned continuously for 300 years. Out of service for centuries but later encased in granite and reactivated, it is probably the world's oldest lighthouse.

Later the Italians took the lead in lighthouse construction, building a tower at Meloria in 1157 and another at Genoa at about the same time. By 1449 the keeper of the Genoa light was Antonio Colombo, whose nephew Christopher Columbus was later to sail forth from Spain for the New World.

As the Turks, Germans, English, and French joined in providing lighthouses along their shores, the structures became more and more ornate. In 1584 Louis de Foix designed a massive lighthouse that was built by the French government on the island of Cordouan. It consisted of a main floor fifty-two feet in diameter, a large second floor housing a chapel, and a tower with a wood-burning lantern and chimney on top. A circular stairway was set off from the main structure, supposedly so the keepers would not dirty the lower rooms as they hauled wood to the top and returned with

To navigate the sounds and waterways of coastal North Carolina with their dugout canoes, Indians relied on familiar landmarks to avoid underwater shoals. John White made these paintings of Indians and their watercraft in the 1580s. (Photos from the files of the Division of Archives and History.)

ashes. Numerous windows, pillars, parapets, statues and other ornaments decorated the main tower.

Famed in song and story, the first Eddystone light was built by the government of Great Britain in 1698 on the Eddystone Rocks, until then a nightmare for navigators. But maintenance of a lighthouse on exposed rocks off the English coast was a nightmare in itself, for the dangerous rocks were alternately exposed and then covered by the waves as the tide rose and fell. During construction members of the work crew were taken prisoner by French privateers, and a year after its completion the light was extinguished in order that the stone base could be strengthened and enlarged and the light raised forty feet. Four years later, while work was under way on further improvements, the lighthouse and all of its occupants were swept away in a violent storm.

So great was the need for a warning light on the Eddystone Rocks, however, that the English persisted, despite failure after failure, to build a lighthouse there. A second Eddystone light, built of stone and wood, was completed in 1708, but it caught fire and burned in 1755; a third one, with twenty-four candles and reflectors providing the light, was completed in 1759 and remained on station for 123 years, when it was dismantled and finally replaced with the structure still located there.

As in so many other activities the Americans were late arrivals in the lighthouse construction business. The Boston light, built in 1716, was the first one in the American colonies; but throughout the colonial period only eleven lighthouses were built in America, nine of them between Delaware Bay and Maine, and the other two at Charleston and Savannah.

The long, exposed, and dangerous coast of North Carolina was without the protection of lighthouses until well after the Revolutionary War.

2

The North Carolina Coast

The Pacific coast of the United States for the most part is rocky and rugged, often with mountains rising almost directly from the sea. Much of our northern Atlantic coast has similar characteristics, with prominent landmarks that look the same today as they did when first sighted by Europeans hundreds of years ago. Further, as a general rule, wherever there are precipitous mountains there are equally precipitous valleys between them, and along such a coastline the valleys frequently extend below the surface of the sea, providing deep natural harbors that are stabilized by the rocky formations around them.

By comparison, much of the extensive Gulf coast of Louisiana is a huge delta formed by silt that has been carried down the Mississippi River through the ages. Similar conditions exist along the lower Atlantic coast, off South Carolina and Georgia, for example, resulting in the formation of vast marshlands, covered with mud and reedlike grass and broken only by the channels of deep rivers flowing through them to the sea.

The geographical formations along the coast of North Carolina claim kinship to the marshlands of Louisiana and South Carolina and Georgia, but with one major difference that sets them apart. The marshlands spreading across much of the North Carolina coastal area terminate in broad inland bodies of water, "sounds," such as Currituck, Pamlico, and Bogue, and they are separated from the Atlantic by a chain of barrier islands—sandy shoals really—rising ever so slightly above the surface. These banks of sand, extending from the Virginia border southward past Cape Hatteras and Cape Lookout to Bogue Inlet, and to a lesser degree on down to the boundary line with South Carolina at Calabash, are known today as the Outer Banks.

The coastline of North Carolina extends for 301 miles, comprising more than a quarter of the total coastline of the thirteen English colonies in America. By coincidence this 301 miles equals exactly the combined coastline of the states of Virginia, Maryland, Delaware, and New Jersey. To put it in a different perspective it is exactly the same distance from our Virginia border to New York as it is from that same border to the South Carolina state line.

John White's map of the Carolina coast in 1585 featured more detail and greater accuracy than any other map of the New World up to that time. Place-names like Chesapeake, Hatteras, and Roanoke appeared for the first time on this map. Reproduced, with permission, from William P. Cumming, *The Southeast in Early Maps* (Chapel Hill: University of North Carolina Press, 1958), plate 12.

Though the North Carolina coastline was longer than that of any of the other twelve original states, almost all of the others were blessed with far superior deepwater ports. Even Pennsylvania, an interior state with only eighty-nine miles of estuarine shoreline (compared with more than 3,000 miles of such interior shores in North Carolina) and none at all on the Atlantic coast, offered easy access for ocean-going vessels entering Delaware Bay en route to the Philadelphia area.

Because so much of the extensive North Carolina coastline is low and relatively flat, without distinguishing landmarks or permanent highlands, the early explorers had great difficulty in determining exactly where they were. This posed special problems in locating the narrow inlets that provided access to the interior waters and in avoiding the dangerous underwater shoals that stretched seaward from Cape Hatteras, Cape Lookout, and Cape Fear.

Skirting ocean shoals and locating the half-hidden inlets along the coast were just the beginning of the problems faced by mariners during the period of early settlement. The existence of a vast network of rivers and creeks thrusting westward from the broad coastal sounds made overland transportation both difficult and impractical, thus calling for dependence on sea-borne commerce as a means of bringing in the needed supplies to the North Carolina settlers and of exporting raw materials. Yet almost all of these interior or estuarine waters were shallow, with the channels constantly shoaling and shifting.

The only exceptions were the Cape Fear River, on the lower coast, and Old Topsail Inlet, which provided access to the port of Beaufort near Cape Lookout.

Even the Cape Fear River, North Carolina's single deepwater channel leading to the interior, offered extreme hazards for navigators. Approaching the mouth of the river from the sea they first had to avoid Frying Pan Shoals, whose massive sandy tentacles stretched out from Cape Fear, and then encounter a veritable honeycomb of ever shifting channels, shoals, and sand bars before reaching deep water in the river itself.

Old Topsail was probably the most stable harbor on the coast, but once a vessel reached safe anchorage at Beaufort that was about as far as it could go, for there was absolutely no access from Port Beaufort to any sounds or rivers of consequence.

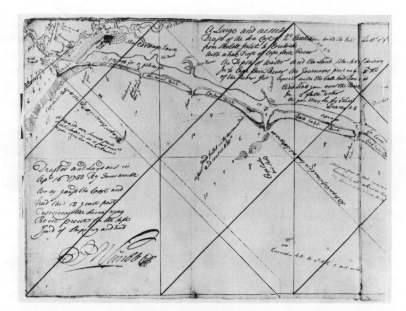

This map of the North Carolina coast, drafted by mariner and plantation owner James Wimble in 1733, featured particularly detailed information on the lower Cape Fear and on the shallow water depths all along the Outer Banks. (Photo from the files of the Division of Archives and History.)

Unfortunately, the Cape Fear River and Old Topsail Inlet served only a small proportion of the colonists who settled in North Carolina, for to a large degree they were concentrated in the northern area, in the vicinity of Edenton and Bath and New Bern, all located on tributaries of Albemarle and Pamlico sounds. This was where most early North Carolinians lived, and this was where efforts were concentrated to improve navigation.

The early North Carolinians faced these problems and came up with practical and sometimes ingenious methods of coping with them. For one thing, wherever possible, they carried on their commerce in smaller ocean-going craft that were sometimes specially designed with shallow enough draft to enable them to navigate the sounds and rivers. More and more, however, they devised a system of bringing the larger cargo vessels through the inlets and transferring the cargo to smaller and lighter craft—generally known as lighters—for distribution of cargo throughout the network of estuarine waters.

Even then, however, they constantly faced the prospect of shipwreck, first in the inlets where the channels were in a constant process of change—both in direction and in depth—and later in the sounds and rivers where it was equally difficult to distinguish deep water from hidden sand bars.

Still other problems plagued those engaged in early maritime commerce, not the least being the threat of attack by pirates or privateers. The infamous Blackbeard and Stede Bonnet were two of the pirates who moved their base of operations from the Caribbean to the Carolinas in the early 1700s. Their nefarious activites no doubt were made easier by the unreliability of escape routes for their prospective victims and by the sanctuary the sandy banks afforded them.

Throughout the colonial period there were repeated efforts to provide navigational improvements. The colonial assembly depended on coastal pilots to place markers on the most dangerous shoals and to maintain them, but it typically regulated the watermen's activities by allowing only authorized pilots to board vessels and by setting the rates they could charge.

With ever increasing commerce through Ocracoke Inlet, pilotage became a potentially lucrative profession, and those early pilots who had established a base on Ocracoke saw their livelihood and their integrity threatened by outside competitors. A special concern of the so-called "legal pilots of Oacock Bar," as expressed in a petition to Governor Josiah Martin in 1773, was the intrusion of "sundry Negroes, as well free men as slaves" who had taken it "upon themselves to pilot vessels from Oacock Bar up the several rivers to Bath, Edenton and New Bern, and back again to the said Bar . . . contrary to law." Contending that "great confusion and irregularity daily insue from the insolent and turbilent disposition and behaviour of such free negroes and slaves," the white pilots were rewarded with assurances from the governor that he would do his best to correct the situation.

On several occasions laws were passed that levied charges against every vessel entering a North Carolina port, with a portion of the proceeds designated for marking channels. But few shoals or channels were marked, and even when they were it was not unusual for the buoys or markers to be swept away by wind or tide during the first hard blow.

By the 1770s and the coming of the American Revolution, pilots had located at most of the navigable inlets, and at isolated Ocracoke Island they had built semipermanent shacks to form a community known as Pilot Town on the approximate site of the present-day village of Ocracoke. But compared with the coast of Europe, or even the more northern coast of America, North Carolina was unguarded, and the mariner approaching its shores was forced to rely almost exclusively on his ability, judgment, and luck.

3

The First North Carolina Lighthouses

When independence came at last to the thirteen British colonies in America and they joined together in a federation of united states, it was impossible to spell out in detail exactly where the individual state's rights ended and the federal government's rights began. In the construction of lighthouses, as in so many other instances, the final answer was not based on political considerations or even on the wishes of the people or their elected representatives. Rather, the compelling and deciding factor was: Who will pay the bills?

The state of North Carolina took a crack at the lighthouse construction business early on, initiating independent efforts to provide lighthouses at the entrance to the two major ports, Ocracoke and the Cape Fear River.

Bald Head, a distinctive mound of sand on a large island located on the southeast side of the mouth of the Cape Fear River, was selected as the site of the first North Carolina lighthouse. In order to finance the project the General Assembly of the new state passed an act in 1784 levying an additional sixpence per ton duty on all vessels entering the Cape Fear River, the proceeds to be set aside for construction of the proposed lighthouse at Bald Head.

Typically in such cases, several prominent individuals were named as commissioners of navigation with responsibility for holding the money collected by the special duty, acquiring a site for the lighthouse, and arranging for building the structure. Though detailed information is scarce, it appears that the efforts of the commissioners were beset with difficulties from the outset.

The site under consideration was owned by Benjamin Smith, a longtime member of the assembly, early benefactor of the University of North Carolina, and later governor of the state, who offered to donate ten acres of high land on a promontory on Bald Head overlooking both the river and the sea. Smith seemed greatly concerned, however, that people visiting his isolated island, both during and after construction of the lighthouse, might steal or kill his cattle and hogs, and special action by the assembly was required to provide the protection for which he asked.

It was not until the session of 1789 that the assembly enacted legislation that added Smith to the "commissioners of pilotage for the bar and river of Cape Fear" and further prohibited any person from keeping "cattle, hogs and stock of any kind" on Smith's Island. A single exception to this general prohibition, inserted in the state law, permitted the individual named as keeper of the lighthouse to keep poultry, plus one cow and one calf for his personal use. An even more stringent regulation was that no one was permitted to hunt on the island without specific permission from Smith, and any person found on Smith's Island with a gun "or other hunting instruments" was subject to a stiff fine.

There are clear indications in the 1789 act that the commissioners had already begun construction of the lighthouse on Smith's ten acres. Further confirmation of this came on November 27 of that year when a committee of the House of Representatives reported that the Cape Fear commissioners had contracted with a man named Thomas Withers to deliver 200,000 bricks to Bald Head "for the purpose of erecting a lighthouse," but because his vessels had become stranded, as well as other circumstances, he had sustained considerable loss. The committeemen recommended that they be allowed to increase the price paid Withers to four pounds and fifteen shillings, which was considerably higher than the original contract price, but which they insisted was "the average price of bricks since purchased by them for the completion of said lighthouse."

The same 1789 sesssion of the assembly that had provided Smith with special protection from cattle thieves and hunters at Bald Head and had seemed anxious to bail out Thomas Withers from his ill-fated contract to provide brick for the lighthouse there also took action designed to provide a second state lighthouse, this one at Ocracoke.

The specific legislation was an "Act to Erect a Light-house on Ocacock Island." (In those days spelling of the name "Ocracoke" was inconsistent, ranging from "Okok" to "Ocacock" to "Okercoke.") The preamble to the act acknowledged that construction of a lighthouse on the island "would tend greatly to the safety of vessels bound over Ocacock Bar, and very much encourage foreigners as well as citizens of the United States to trade with this State." The act named seven "commissioners for erecting a lighthouse on Ocacock Island" and provided for a special duty on any vessel of twenty tons or more crossing Ocracoke Bar—threepence per ton "on all vessels belonging to this or any of the United States" and twice as much, sixpence per ton, "upon all foreign vessels." The duty was to be paid to the collectors of the ports of Currituck, Roanoke, Bath, and Beaufort.

The Ocracoke commissioners were also instructed to pick out an appropriate site for the proposed Ocracoke lighthouse, not to exceed one acre in size, and to attempt to secure a deed either by purchase or by gift. This appears to have been the easiest part of their assigned duties, for on November 19, 1789, Governor Alexander Martin transmitted to the General Assembly "a deed of gift of an acre of land on Ocracoke Island, granted by Mess. William Williams, John Williams, Joseph Williams and William Howard, Junior, proprietors of said land, to the Governor of this State and his successors, for the purpose of erecting thereon a light-house, pursuant to an act of the Assembly passed at the last session."

Even as these activities were taking place at Fayetteville and Bald Head and Ocracoke, however, the Congress of the United States was in the process of taking action of its own to relieve the individual states of responsibility for building and maintaining lighthouses. On August 7, 1789, the Congress passed a far-reaching act "for the establishment and support of light-houses, beacons, buoys

The first North Carolina lighthouse was erected on Bald Head Island at the mouth of the Cape Fear River. This sketch of a water spout at the entrance of the Cape Fear, made in 1805, included the Bald Head light. (From the files of the Division of Archives and History.)

and public piers." It provided that after August 15, 1789, all expenses for the maintenance and repair of such structures built or under construction by the states should be "defrayed out of the Treasury of the United States," thus effectively transferring responsibility for construction of lighthouses and other aids to navigation from the states to the federal government, a policy that has remained in effect ever since.

A specific provision of the federal act was that all such structures, and the land on which they were located, were to be deeded to the United States, and in 1790 the North Carolina General Assembly passed legislation requiring the governor to transfer both the Bald Head and the Ocracoke lighthouse sites to the federal government.

Though Congress failed to appropriate funds for lighthouses in its 1789 act, it did instruct the secretary of the treasury to prepare contracts for repairing existing lighthouses and for building a new one at the entrance to Chesapeake Bay. In its next session in 1790 Congress appropriated funds for building the Chesapeake Bay light and for completing a Maine lighthouse already under construction on Portland Head. Finally, in 1792 "a sum, not exceeding four thousand dollars," was appropriated to finish construction of the Bald Head lighthouse at the mouth of the Cape Fear River. The fact that only four thousand dollars was considered necessary to complete the Bald Head light strongly indicates that the state had almost finished construction, because the initial appropriation for building the Chesapeake Bay lighthouse from the ground up amounted to "one hundred and forty-seven thousand one hundred and sixty nine dollars and fifty four cents."

The work of completing the Bald Head lighthouse proceeded slowly, in part at least because the original cost estimates were too low and Congress had to make three additional appropriations, totaling more than seven thousand dollars, before the structure could be completed and finally lighted in 1795.

At long last, with the federal government picking up where the state had left off, North Carolina had its first lighthouse, though there were almost immediate complaints that it was inadequate, not only in warning vessels away from the dangerous Frying Pan Shoals, but also in providing guidance for mariners seeking to enter the Cape Fear River.

Even before the Bald Head lighthouse was completed Congress took steps to provide navigational aids at the other main port of entry, Ocracoke Inlet. The need there, however, was quite different. The primary dangers at Cape Fear were the massive underwater shoals stretching out into the sea from Bald Head and the narrow, winding channels at the mouth of the river. At Ocracoke, on the other hand, ocean-going vessels had relatively little difficulty approaching and entering Ocracoke Inlet; but once they crossed the bar they were confronted with a labyrinth of shoals and shallow channels, ever changing in location and in size.

Though the federal government had already received title to the one-acre state lighthouse site on Ocracoke Island, Congress disregarded that location and turned its attention to the area just back of Ocracoke Inlet in Pamlico Sound. A 1793 act directed Secretary of the Treasury Alexander Hamilton to provide "a beacon or floating buoy at the southwest straddle, on the Royal Shoal," a key location for any vessel passing through Ocracoke Inlet into the sound. There has been a succession of navigational aids including light vessels, lighthouses, and automated lighting devices in essentially the same location ever since.

By the 1790s Ocracoke Inlet had become a bustling maritime center. The town of Portsmouth, on the south side of the inlet, was the largest on the northern North Carolina coast, while across the inlet, on the north side, the future community of Ocracoke was beginning to take on a distinctive character of its own. But the most unusual development was taking place on a barren island called Old Rock in Pamlico Sound between Royal Shoal and the inlet. Old Rock in reality was a massive bed of oyster shells, half a mile in length but only twenty yards or so in width, its top layer of shells alternately submerged and exposed as the inlet tide rose and fell.

Old Rock was one of five islands near Ocracoke Inlet purchased in 1789 by John Wallace of Portsmouth and John Gray Blount of Washington, the latter a prosperous merchant and shipowner with a small fleet of vessels operating out of the Pamlico River community. Changing the name of Old Rock to Shell Castle Island, they embarked on an ambitious project to construct a major shipping center there in the open sound by providing facilities for ocean-going vessels to unload their cargo for transshipment by

Shell Castle lighthouse, on a tiny island between Ocracoke Inlet and Pamlico Sound, was illuminated around 1800. "Governor" John Wallace and John Gray Blount, owners of the island, ran a thriving business there until shifting shoals ruined it as a deepwater port. This rendering of the Shell Castle beacon appeared on a vase owned by the Blount family and now in the possession of the North Carolina Museum of History.

lighters and other small craft to the increasingly populous northern counties of North Carolina served by the interior ports of New Bern, Bath, and Edenton.

The distinctive feature of Shell Castle that made it especially suitable for their purposes was that it was, literally, a rock: a stable mass of interwoven layers of oyster shells, quite different from the exposed sand bars or marshy islands so typical of the surrounding area. Its location, immediately adjacent to the deepest part of the channel leading from Ocracoke Inlet to the sound, made it possible for large vessels to tie up at the wharves Wallace and Blount built there.

The initial construction phase at Shell Castle produced a warehouse, gristmill and windmill, and living quarters for the people residing on the island, in addition to the wharves. Shortly a store was added, and plans were made for establishing a ship chandlery, a lumber yard, extensive cisterns, residences, and eventually a tavern. In a single decade the facilities had become so extensive that the main building was reported to be 300 feet long, and Wallace and Blount had branched out into a number of related sidelines, operating a fishery, providing lighters, and fairly well controlling pilotage through Ocracoke Inlet. John Wallace, the operating partner, carried on the business in the manner of a feudal ruler, gaining in the process the informal title of "Governor" of Shell Castle.

Congress took cognizance of these activities and in May, 1794, authorized construction "on an island in the harbor of Ocracoke called Shell Castle, a lighted beacon, of wooden frame, fifty-five feet high, to be twenty-two feet at the base, and to be reduced gradually to twelve feet at the top, exclusive of the lantern, which shall be made to contain one large lamp, with four wicks."

The lot Wallace and Blount deeded to the government for the lighthouse on Shell Castle Island was only forty feet wide and 140 feet long. Yet it was large enough to accommodate a twelve-by-twenty-foot dwelling for the lighthouse keeper in addition to the pyramid-shaped, shingle-covered tower on which the light was located.

The exact date on which the Shell Castle lighthouse was first illuminated is not presently known, though it is variously reported as early as 1798 or as late as 1803. Regardless of when it was first lighted, the Shell Castle light, built wholly at federal expense, at long last provided mariners serving the great bulk of the residents of North Carolina with the type of navigational aid they had unsuccessfully sought from the government of North Carolina, both as a colony and as a state, for nearly a century.

With lighthouses at Bald Head as well as at Shell Castle, the two primary North Carolina ports were equipped with recognizable and distinctive landmarks, by night as well as by day.

4

Guarding the Coast

One of the world's major shipping lanes passes just off the east coast of the United States, connecting the maritime centers of the Middle Atlantic and New England states with the Caribbean, the Gulf of Mexico, and South America. Today there is a constant flow of traffic on this highway of the sea, mostly tankers and freighters but with a sprinkling of fishing vessels, brightly lighted cruise ships and other pleasure craft, and a growing number of contrabands smuggling marijuana and cocaine. Almost without exception they are equipped with highly sophisticated equipment—radar, sonar, and loran, to cite a few—designed to assist navigators in determining their location, in setting their course, and in avoiding shoals and other underwater obstructions. But it was not always so.

True, this coastal shipping lane has existed since the earliest days of American colonization, and because the sailing vessels of those earlier years were so much smaller than those of today, it is entirely possible that at any given time back then there were more ships off the coast than there are today. But, lacking the complicated on-board navigational aids that modern technology has developed, each of those early vessels embarked on a hazardous adventure every time it put to sea, and at no place was the journey more hazardous than off the coast of North Carolina.

The first effort by the federal Congress to heed the constant call of coastal captains for navigational aids specifically designed to assist vessels passing offshore came in 1794 in the same act that authorized the "lighted beacon" at Shell Castle. The secretary of the treasury, the act provided, was to proceed with plans for construction of a lighthouse "of the first rate" to be located on the "head-land of Cape Hatteras."

It is impossible to understand the importance of Cape Hatteras to the early commerce of the United States without first gaining a basic knowledge of the geography of the southern coast and of the major ocean currents that pass off these shores.

There is a common misconception that the coast below Cape Hatteras continues to run in a southerly direction, when in fact it trends considerably more to the west than to the south. Jacksonville, on the Florida coast, for example, is less than 300 miles south of Cape Hatteras, but more than 300 miles to the west; and if you

were to sail due south from Hatteras the first land you would encounter would be Cat Island in the Bahamas, which is almost due
east of the southernmost point in the United States, Key West. As a
result, all vessels hugging the coast, as most of them did in the early
days of sail, must make an abrupt change in course at Cape Hatteras.

Making such a change in course, however, involved much more
than just turning the wheel and resetting the sails, for Hatteras is
the point where the two major ocean currents off the East Coast,
the northbound Gulf Stream and the southbound remnant of the
Labrador Current, collide head on. This collision causes constant
turbulence off Cape Hatteras and has resulted in the formation of a
shifting mass of underwater sand bars that stretch eastward into
the Atlantic from the cape for some fourteen miles, creating Diamond Shoals, dreaded by mariners the world over.

The passage around Cape Hatteras was especially difficult for
southbound sailing vessels, for it was there at the outer edge of the
Diamond that they encountered the warm waters of the Gulf
Stream, a veritable ocean river moving northward at a sustained
speed of approximately four miles per hour. And if this hazard had
not been enough, the prevailing wind in the area is from the southwest, forcing vessels to back up north of the cape, unable for days to
overcome the combined force of the Gulf Stream and the south-
westerly winds. Even as recently as the beginning of this century
old-timers living at Kinnakeet just north of Cape Hatteras could
remember seeing as many as 150 "sails of vessels" tacking back and
forth, waiting for the wind to change, and hoping to avoid wrecking
on the shoals when such a shift finally came. Even in daylight under
the best of sailing conditions it was difficult for the mariner to know
when he was in danger of piling up on Diamond Shoals. At night
the first warning he was likely to receive was the ominous sound of
the breakers on the shoals themselves.

Despite the importance the federal government attached to providing a lighthouse at this strategic point, it was not until 1802,
eight years after the original congressional authorization, that the
Cape Hatteras lighthouse was completed, and even then it was
another year before the oil lamps could be installed and the light
placed in operation.

It must have been an imposing structure, that first Cape Hat-

The first Cape Hatteras lighthouse, completed in 1802, stood until 1871. Union forces camped around it in 1861. (Photo from the files of the Division of Archives and History.)

teras lighthouse, its natural sandstone tower rising ninety feet above the bare beach. It was supported by a stone foundation sunk thirteen feet into the sand, the whole structure topped by a ten-foot-high enclosure that housed the lantern and illuminating devices.

The site chosen for the lighthouse, four acres, belonged to William Jennett, Mary Jennett, Jabez Jennett, and Aquilla Jennett, described as "infants under the age of twenty-one years, to whom Christian Jennett, their mother, hath been duly appointed guardian." The purchase price tendered by the United States government, referred to as a "liberal offer," was "twelve and a half dollars an acre, amounting to fifty dollars," but a special act of the North Carolina General Assembly was required in order to finalize the transfer, and that act was not ratified until 1800.

A two-story house, with a cellar, was built for the keeper, and oil was stored in a vault measuring twenty by twelve feet in size and containing nine cedar cisterns, each with a capacity of 200 gallons. Wooden stairs within the stone structure provided access to the tower and the gallery on which the lantern was located, and in 1806 it was described by a visitor as "a handsome plain edifice well calculated for the purpose, and an excellent piece of masonry." However, the same visitor, a man named William Tatham, called it "an architectural Eye Sore" because it was made of two kinds of stone and reported that some cracks were developing, probably because the structure was "too ponderous for the nature of the foundation." Still another problem reported by Tatham was that the heat from the lamp was so intense that the keeper frequently had to jump backward while working in the area, and on more than one such occasion he had struck and broken the glass surrounding the gallery.

A variety of reasons have been advanced for the slow pace of construction on this badly needed light tower. For one thing, Congress took its time making funds available, delaying the initial appropriation until 1797, three years after passage of the act authorizing construction. The contractor was a former congressman, Henry Dearborn, for whom the Michigan city was later named, and the fact that he was also awarded the contract for construction of the beacon at Shell Castle Island could have been a factor.

There are indications that a number of the workmen Dearborn imported for the job suffered from a common illness, possibly malaria, but the basic reason for the slow pace of construction can probably be attributed to the fact that all of the sandstone and other building materials had to be brought to the cape by boat, unloaded without benefit of a decent harbor or wharves, and then transported again across the sandy beach to the building site.

With the completion of the Cape Hatteras lighthouse two of North Carolina's three capes and associated offshore shoals, Cape Fear and Cape Hatteras, were marked with lighthouses; and two of its three ports, the Cape Fear River and Ocracoke, were similarly served. Unmarked still was Cape Lookout and the adjacent inlet, Old Topsail, which served as the deepwater channel to the port of Beaufort.

The initial authorization "for building a lighthouse on or near the pitch of Cape Lookout" was included in an 1804 congressional act. A four-acre site at the cape was deeded to the government in February, 1805, by Joseph Fulford and Elijah Pigott, though it appears construction was not begun for several more years.

In 1806 in the course of a survey of the North Carolina coast for

Secretary of the Treasury Albert Gallatin, William Tatham was instructed to inspect the cape area with care and pick a site for the proposed lighthouse. He came up with the idea of building it atop one of several high sandhills, ranging from twenty to forty-seven feet in elevation according to his calculations, which were located in close proximity to Cape Lookout. Either his recommendation failed to reach the key decision makers in Washington, or it was dismissed as impractical, for the site on which the lighthouse was finally built was the original four-acre Fulford-Pigott tract.

Official records of the federal lighthouse establishment give 1812 as the year the structure was completed. Though no detailed contemporary description appears to exist, it was later listed as being ninety-six feet high and described as consisting of two towers: "the inside one is brick—the outside one is a wooden framed building, boarded and shingled, and painted in red and white stripes horizontally."

Even as the Cape Lookout lighthouse was being completed, bringing to four the number of coastal North Carolina lighthouses built by the federal government, complaints were being heard about the inadequacy of the first two, the Bald Head lighthouse at Cape Fear and the Shell Castle light at Ocracoke Inlet.

The problem at Bald Head was that there had been such a drastic change in the Cape Fear River channel that the light could no longer be seen by most vessels making their way from the river to the open sea. Specifically, as has happened so frequently during the intervening years all along the coast, a new inlet had opened, some eight miles to the north of Bald Head, thereby providing a more direct connection between the Cape Fear and the Atlantic Ocean. Actually, in almost all instances, these cuts through the Outer Banks are opened and kept open by the force of water coursing down creeks and rivers from the mountains and through the Piedmont and the Coastal Plain seeking an outlet to the sea. Thus, they are outlets rather than inlets, and an old maxim on the coast is when natural forces choose to change the location of a channel man had best accept the change and leave well enough alone.

In the Cape Fear case more and more mariners used the new inlet in preference to the meandering channel at the mouth of the river for which the Bald Head lighthouse had been built, and it became obvious that new navigational aids should be provided as a guide to vessels using the recently opened inlet.

The original congressional authorization in 1814 was for the construction of a beacon to be located at Federal Point on the north side of the New Inlet. Official lighthouse records list 1816 as the year in which the Federal Point lighthouse was put in service.

The contemporary observer might have assumed that the construction of the fifty-foot-high Federal Point lighthouse at New Inlet had solved the major navigational problems on the lower Cape Fear, but such was not the case. For the other Cape Fear lighthouse, the one at Bald Head on Smith Island, was so severely threatened by shore-front erosion that it seemed to be on the verge of toppling over, and plans were made for replacing it with a new lighthouse structure located well back from the water. This second Bald Head lighthouse, an octagonal structure, was constructed of bricks with an exterior coating of cement. Completed in 1818 at a cost of $15,915.45, it exhibited a light 109 feet above the water level. Known affectionately as "Old Baldy," it sits on a bluff near the edge of Smith Island's extensive northern marshes, surrounded still by magnificient live oaks, the remnants of Bald Head's maritime forest. Long since deactivated, "Old Baldy" is the oldest standing lighthouse structure in North Carolina.

Meanwhile, at Shell Castle, a combination of circumstances had made necessary the replacement of the lighthouse there. A violent storm in 1806 caused considerable damage to the Wallace-Blount facilities at Shell Castle. "Governor" John Wallace, the driving force behind the operation, died in 1810 without having designated an heir apparent to carry on the business. But it remained for nature to deal the final blow, a two-pronged attack that began with the gradual shoaling of the channel adjacent to the wharves and the opening of a major new channel more than a mile away, rendering the Shell Castle facility all but useless. The climax was a report in 1818 that both the lighthouse and the keeper's quarters had been struck by lightning and destroyed.

Despite the change in the channel Congress appropriated $14,000 in 1820 for "a light-house on Shell Castle island, in the State of North Carolina, or, in lieu thereof, a light-vessel, to be moored in a proper place, near the said island, if, in the opinion of the Secretary of Treasury, the latter shall be preferred." The light vessel was preferred by the secretary, but it apparently proved in-

When the Shell Castle beacon became inoperative, the federal government built the Ocracoke lighthouse in 1823. Shown here are the light station and dwelling house in 1893. (Photos from the files of the U.S. Coast Guard.)

effective. Two years later an additional $20,000 was appropriated for construction of a new lighthouse on Ocracoke Island, and the floating light was removed.

The Ocracoke lighthouse, measuring sixty-five feet from ground level to the center of the light, was completed and illuminated in 1823 and is still in service, making it the oldest operating lighthouse on the North Carolina coast.

The Ocracoke lighthouse was built by Noah Porter of Massachusetts at a total cost of $11,359.35 including construction of a one-bedroom keeper's quarters. The deed for the original one-acre Ocracoke lighthouse site acquired by the state more than thirty years earlier had contained a reversion clause that rendered it void if a lighthouse were not built on the site by 1801. It was therefore necessary for the government to acquire a new site for the lighthouse that had been authorized in 1822, and in December of that year a two-acre site was purchased from Jacob Gaskill for fifty dollars.

Thus, in 1823, a third of a century after the United States Congress had assumed responsibility for the construction and maintenance of lighthouses and other aids to navigation, the four most important points on the North Carolina coast—Cape Hatteras, Ocracoke Inlet, Cape Lookout, and Cape Fear—were marked with distinctive towers and modern lights.

5

Light Vessels

Question: How do you put a lighthouse on a dangerous sub-merged shoal so far out to sea that it is often beyond the sight of land? This was the problem Congress addressed initially in 1806 when it appropriated $5,000 for a survey of the North Carolina coast to determine the practicability of erecting lighthouses on the shoals that stretched seaward from Cape Hatteras, Cape Lookout, and Cape Fear.

The key location was Diamond Shoals, off Cape Hatteras, for mariners were complaining already that the beam from the new Cape Hatteras lighthouse was seldom visible on the outer fringes of the shoals. More than a century and a half later engineers were finally able to solve the problem by placing the lighthouses on top of elevated stilt-legged towers of the type designed for offshore oil drilling. But in the early 1800s neither the technology nor the equipment was available for such an undertaking, and the survey party concluded that there was little chance that a lighthouse could remain intact for long on the shoals, even if one could be built there.

In the ensuing decades, however, the United States government experimented with an alternate solution: in effect building the lighthouses on top of floating vessels firmly anchored near the danger spots. The term generally used to identify these floating lighthouses was "light vessels," though most often the smaller ones used in interior waters were known as "light boats" and the larger offshore craft as "lightships."

The first American light vessel, a seventy-ton craft, was placed on duty in 1820 at Willoughby Spit near Norfolk, Virginia. The following year another survey party examined the shoals off the North Carolina capes and recommended the placement of a light vessel on Diamond Shoals. Larger vessels obviously were needed for these "outside stations," as they were called, and in March, 1823, Congress authorized the expenditure of $25,000 for construc-tion of a vessel for the shoals off Cape Hatteras, specifying that it was "not to be under two hundred and fifty tons." At that time lighthouses were the responsibility of the fifth auditor of the United States Treasury, a zealous guardian of public funds named Stephen Pleasanton, who in short order contracted with New York

shipbuilder Henry Eckford for construction of the Cape Hatteras vessel.

With a displacement of 300 tons, that first Diamond Shoals lightship was more than four times as large as the original Willoughby Spit lightboat. It was equipped with two lights, each one encased in a three-foot-square lantern five feet tall and mounted high up on the vessel's masts, one light being sixty feet above the water level and the other fifteen feet lower. The lanterns had been designed especially for the Diamond Shoals lightship by Commodore James Barron (otherwise noted for having killed Stephen Decatur in a duel), whose fee was $550 for the work.

In April, 1824, Captain Christian Erickson of Philadelphia was appointed master of the vessel, with a mate and four crewmen serving under him. Captain Erickson had understood that he was to receive a salary of $800 per year, but in June Congress reduced this to $700 and set the mate's pay at half that amount. Though there is no record of how much the four seamen were paid, it is known that an allowance of twenty-five cents per man per day was provided for rations.

As so often happens there was a shadowy figure working behind the scenes as the saga of the Diamond Shoals lightship unfolded. This was a naval officer, a Captain Jesse Elliott, apparently a confidant of the fifth auditor, who had been influential in securing the congressional appropriation and had inspected the vessel for Pleasanton during the course of construction. After the lightship had been launched and was ready to put to sea on its maiden voyage in late June, 1824, Captain Elliott volunteered to sail on the voyage as a passenger. What happened between Captain Erickson, the master of the vessel, and Captain Elliott the passenger as the craft sailed down the coast and took up its station at a point thirteen miles east-southeast of Cape Hatteras unfortunately is not known. Immediately upon his return, however, Elliott wrote to Pleasanton and complained among other things about Captain Erickson's "intemperate conduct." Consequently, Erickson was

Facing page: Early attempts to station a light vessel at Diamond Shoals in the 1820s proved futile. *Diamond Shoals Lightship 69* finally took up its vigil in 1897, but two years later a storm drove it ashore at Cape Hatteras. In 1918 the Diamond Shoals lightship was ignominiously sunk by a German submarine. (Upper photo from the files of the U.S. Coast Guard; lower photo from the library of David Stick.)

promptly relieved of duty, and in July the announcement was made that he had been replaced as master of the Diamond Shoals lightship by Captain Lief Holden.

Any vessel anchored for long off Diamond Shoals is bound to have a stormy career, but no one could have anticipated just how stormy and how ineffective would be the relatively short career of the first Diamond Shoals lightship. In February, 1825, just eight months after arriving at its station off Cape Hatteras, the ship parted its moorings in a violent storm, though Captain Holden somehow managed to avoid stranding on the nearby shoals and finally sailed his craft to Norfolk for repairs. In addition to the loss of the massive anchor and cable the damage must have been extensive, for the estimated cost of the repairs was $12,000, nearly half the original construction cost of the lightship. Worse still, the repair work proceeded at an abnormally slow pace, and it was December before she was back on duty again, equipped this time with a six-pound cannon undoubtedly for use as a fog signal.

There can be no more than speculation on what life was like for Captain Holden and his mate and four seamen on their floating lighthouse at the isolated station off Cape Hatteras in the winter of 1825-1826, for these were not men inclined to put their thoughts in writing. Certainly it could have been no better, and probably was worse, than life on larger and more modern lightships at other isolated stations many decades later, of which written records have been preserved. Frequently, the crew remained on board for months on end without relief and in fact without contact of any sort with other human beings, unless seeing figures on the decks of passing ships through a spyglass can be classed as contact. It was "the terrors of isolation" even more than "the perils of wind and wave" that made so many first-timers curse the day they came aboard and accounted for an exceptionally high turnover of crewmen.

One bitter sailor described life on a lightship as "a term of solitary confinement combined with the horrors of sea-sickness," and the comparison with a jail sentence almost certainly comes to mind for anyone who has ever boarded a light vessel. One veteran crewman put it this way: "If it weren't for the disgrace it would bring to my family I'd rather go to State's Prison."

In later years it was general practice for the crew to be divided into two shifts, one headed by the captain and the other by the mate, and for each to spend approximately four months ashore each year. These periods of extended leave began in the early spring and lasted through the fall, which meant that the full crew would be on board during the worst months in the dead of winter. It is doubtful that any such system was in effect in the 1820s when the first American light vessels went into service, but even without a regular schedule of annual leave those aboard the Diamond Shoals lightship spent more than their fair share of time ashore.

In May, 1826, only five months after returning to the Cape Hatteras station, Captain Holden was again forced to put to sea when his cables broke in a severe storm, and as before he was able to sail the lightship back to Norfolk. On learning of the mishap Fifth Auditor Pleasanton, always the protector of the people's pocketbook, ordered Captain Holden to engage another vessel and return to the scene in an attempt to locate and recover the lost anchor and cable. When this effort proved fruitless, Pleasanton offered a $500 reward to anyone who could recover the anchor and cable, while the lightship, once more ready for duty, remained at a berth in Norfolk for five additional months. When the reward money failed to produce results, a Baltimore firm was finally employed to build a new anchor. In November, 1826, the lightship returned to her lonely vigil off Diamond Shoals.

The end came ten months later, in August, 1827, when for the third time the Diamond Shoals lightship broke loose in a storm. This time, however, Captain Holden was unable to save the vessel. A total loss, it ended up on the beach at Ocracoke, just one more name in the long list of casualties in the Graveyard of the Atlantic.

In the twenty-eight months since first anchoring off Diamond Shoals, the ill-fated lightship had left the station unguarded twice—for ten months the first time and for five the second. How many vessels searching for the warning lights that were not there ended up on the shoals or on the beach during those fifteen months will never be known. But the conclusion of all involved seemed to be that it was better to have no lightship stationed there than to have a phantom vessel on duty one day but gone the next. It was to be seventy years before there was another effort to place a lightship off Cape Hatteras.

Meanwhile, undeterred by the Diamond Shoals fiasco, Pleasanton and his associates began to press forward with a determined program to provide smaller lightboats at stations throughout the interior waters of North Carolina. An appropriation of $10,000 was made in 1824 "for a light-vessel to be placed at or near the Long Shoals, on Pamtico Sound, in the State of North Carolina." In rapid succession thereafter other light vessels were authorized, most as replacements for floating buoys, at strategic points in the North Carolina sounds and rivers, with the result that five of them were in service by 1828, and four more by 1836.

Because they ride constantly at anchor, held in place by a long cable or hawser attached to the bow, all light vessels share some common characteristics. Of necessity they must be built high in the bow, for a taut cable has a tendency to pull the bow down and directly into oncoming waves. Described more than once as "sitting ducks" because they are unable to maneuver out of the way of oncoming vessels and thus are frequently rammed, light vessels must be built with thick sides and hulls—"heavily timbered" is the seafaring term. Above all else they must be compact, for these stubby yet ponderous looking craft are both home and workshop to their crewmen through all seasons.

Under certain conditions, and especially in a cross sea, any vessel will pitch (rock from bow to stern) or roll (from side to side), but light vessels have movements all their own. One observer, referring to a lightship as "a tossing island," complained that about the time a person gets accustomed to the pitching and plunging it then begins to rear and roll. To make matters worse lightships sometimes begin plunging while still pitching and rolling while rearing, rather like a horse breaking stride from a gallop to a trot.

The nine lightboats—plus two small lighthouses—put into service at the rate of one a year in North Carolina waters between 1825 and 1836 were designed to provide a network of distinctive day markers and nighttime lights to mark the channels leading from Ocracoke Inlet into Pamlico Sound and fanning out from there in three directions. One route headed toward Core Sound to the south, a second up the Neuse and Pamlico rivers to the west, and the third northward through Croatan and Albemarle sounds to the mouth of the Pasquotank River.

Probably the most important of the new lights was the 140-ton lightboat placed in 1826 on the Southwest Point of Royal Shoal, nine miles from Ocracoke. Vessels bound for the relatively heavy concentrations of population in the vicinity of New Bern on the Neuse River or Washington on the Pamlico headed from Royal Shoal toward a 125-ton lightboat that was stationed on Brant Island Shoal in the middle of Pamlico Sound in 1831. From there they could pick up the Pamtico Point lighthouse located on the south side of the entrance to Pamlico River or the 125-ton lightboat anchored off Marsh Point near the mouth of the Neuse River, both of which were placed in service in 1828. Those headed south into Core Sound were guided by a smaller, seventy-two-ton lightboat, which was stationed at Harbor Island Bar off Cedar Island in 1836.

The four remaining lightboats and a new lighthouse marked the channels to the north. The first one encountered after leaving Ocracoke Inlet was the seventy-ton lightboat stationed at Nine Feet Shoal in 1827 to mark the southern end of the mass of deeper water in Pamlico Sound, a body of landlocked water so vast that early explorers had thought it to be the "western sea," or Pacific Ocean. The trouble is that the deepest waters in Pamlico Sound are still relatively shallow, and at one point near its northern limits a massive shoal extends far out from the mainland for miles, an unanticipated barrier to the mariner not familiar with those waters. This is Long Shoal, and it was at this dangerous spot that the first and largest of the light vessels was placed, the 145-ton Long Shoal lightboat that went in service in 1825.

From Long Shoal northward vessels had to pass through a narrow channel in Croatan Sound separating Roanoke Island from the mainland, and it was decided to put two lights there, one at the south end of Croatan Sound and the other at the north end. The southernmost of these, a lighthouse, was built in 1831 at a point west of the present-day community of Wanchese called Roanoke Marshes; the northernmost one, a seventy-two-ton lightboat, was placed on duty in 1835 and was originally known as the Roanoke Island light vessel, though the name was subsequently changed to Croatan light vessel. Completing the markers for this network of channels from Pamlico Sound through Croatan and Albemarle Sound was the seventy-six-ton Wade's Point Shoal lightboat, which was anchored in Albemarle Sound at the south side of the entrance to the Pasquotank River in 1826.

Though the nine new lightboats varied considerably in size, from 145 tons at Long Shoal to seventy tons at Nine Feet Shoal, all of the lights were approximately the same elevation, forty feet above the water, give or take a couple of feet. The average lightboat crew consisted of a master, a mate, and two to four crewmen, and though some of those hired as lightboat captains were qualified and dedicated mariners, others were reported to be farmers living nearby "who have either employed others at low wages to attend their duties, or wholly neglected them."

The problem at one of the new lighthouses, Roanoke Marshes, was of a different nature, as outlined in an 1842 report by Fifth Auditor Pleasanton. Noting first that the lighthouse, constructed in 1831 by Lucius Lyon of Michigan, "was represented to be very well built," he then went on to explain why it was necessary to abandon it eight years later. He cited three main reasons: "The first was that the place never was fit for the location of a lighthouse, being a low marsh, overflowed at every high tide; and the second was, that the light-house required considerable repairs." But it was the third reason that provided the clincher. The heirs of a man named Van Pelt had obtained a court judgment ordering the ejectment of the keeper from the premises. Van Pelt's heirs claimed ownership of the marsh on which the lighthouse had been built, a fact Pleasanton said was not made known to higher authorities by the agent responsible for supervision of the project.

When the court validated the heirs' claim the government was in the embarrassing position of owning and trying to operate a light on property belonging to private citizens who "asked more than the Treasury was disposed to give" them for the marshy land. Pleasanton's decision was "to abandon the establishment," but apparently soured by the land title experience with Van Pelt's heirs, he made no request at that time for funds with which to provide a replacement.

Pleasanton, who retained full authority over government lighthouses for approximately thirty years, has been much maligned as an auditor without any knowledge of maritime matters. But he must be given credit for providing maritime commerce with a network of lighted navigational aids throughout the vast sound and river waterways of eastern North Carolina, accomplishing in slightly more than a decade what colonial, state, and federal officials had unsuccessfully sought for more than a century.

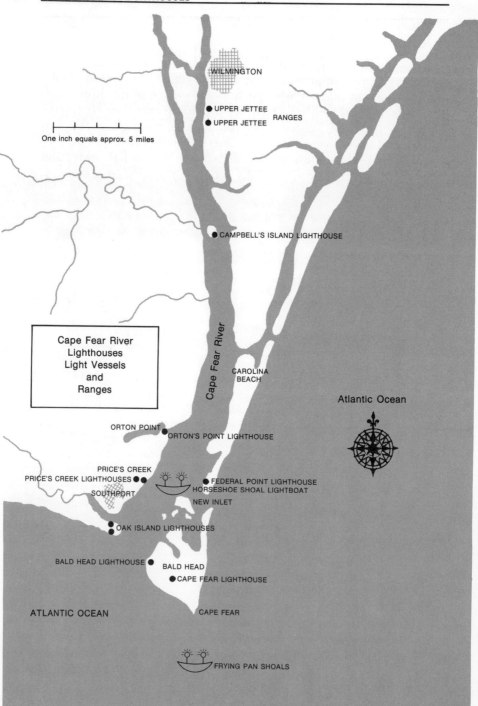

One inch equals approx. 5 miles

WILMINGTON

● UPPER JETTEE
● UPPER JETTEE   RANGES

● CAMPBELL'S ISLAND LIGHTHOUSE

Cape Fear River

Cape Fear River
Lighthouses
Light Vessels
and
Ranges

CAROLINA
BEACH

Atlantic Ocean

ORTON POINT
● ORTON'S POINT LIGHTHOUSE

PRICE'S CREEK
PRICE'S CREEK LIGHTHOUSES ● ●
● FEDERAL POINT LIGHTHOUSE
SOUTHPORT   HORSESHOE SHOAL LIGHTBOAT
NEW INLET

● OAK ISLAND LIGHTHOUSES

BALD HEAD LIGHTHOUSE ●
BALD HEAD
● CAPE FEAR LIGHTHOUSE

ATLANTIC OCEAN   CAPE FEAR

FRYING PAN SHOALS

6

Cape Fear River Lights

North Carolina is laced with a labyrinth of rivers, many beginning as little more than rivulets in the mountains, then forming brooks and creeks and streams as they course eastward toward the sea. Shown flat, on a map, they tend to resemble a stand of small bushy trees, stripped of leaves by winter's harshness, their crooked trunks implanted on the coast, with limbs and branches and twigs spreading out in all directions.

There are thousands of miles of rivers in the state, but only the Cape Fear provides a direct deepwater outlet to the Atlantic Ocean and is thus of major importance in maritime commerce. Early settlers realized the advantages of locating near such a waterway, and one of the first settlements in that part of Carolina was at Brunswick Town on the west bank a few miles upriver from the sea.

As the number of vessels entering the Cape Fear River increased, it was necessary for pilots to locate close enough to the bar to be able to see the sails of incoming craft and quickly offer assistance. Some of the pilots camped on a bluff on the west side of the river at a point where a bend in the natural channel brought deep water close to shore, the site of the present-day Southport. Still later Wilmington replaced Brunswick Town as the major trading center for the river commerce, and it remains today as North Carolina's premier port city.

From the outset those who made use of the Cape Fear River waterway faced the prospect of running aground each time they set sail on the river. There were numerous requests to agents of the government for assistance in providing permanent stakes and beacons to mark the channels in the lower Cape Fear, and on several occasions the colonial assembly imposed duties on incoming vessels as a way of raising money for the purpose, but to little avail. During the course of the Revolutionary War several vessels were sunk in the river, their submerged hulks adding to the navigational hazards. Yet half a century after the war ended, the people of Wilmington were still petitioning Congress to have the wrecks removed or adequately marked.

The reorganization of the lighthouse establishment in 1820 under the direction of Fifth Auditor Stephen Pleasanton had offered

The Bald Head lighthouse could not illuminate the Cape Fear River on its twenty-five-mile course to Wilmington, so during the 1840s various river lights were placed in operation between the port and the river's mouth. (Photo from the files of the U.S. Coast Guard.)

new hope, especially when he began stationing lightboats throughout the upper sounds and rivers, but the Cape Fear did not seem to figure in his early plans. Some no doubt assumed he would turn his attention to the Cape Fear as soon as he had completed the job of marking the main channels leading into the sounds from Ocracoke Inlet, but even after the last of those nine new lightboats was placed on station at Harbor Island Bar in 1836, Pleasanton focused his efforts on other coastal states and ignored the pleas from the Cape Fear area. It was to be twelve more years before the fifth auditor responded to the appeals of the Wilmington merchants and the owners of vessels trading there, but once he had finally decided to do something about aids to navigation on the Cape Fear River, he moved at a rapid pace.

Though it is doubtful anyone in the area today is aware of it, August 14 is a key date worth commemorating; for it was on that day in 1848 that Congress took final action on a bill that provided both the authorization and funding for installation of a series of lights all along the important twenty-five-mile stretch of the Cape Fear River from its mouth to Wilmington.

The appropriation bill, a model that might well be studied by today's lawmakers for its combination of detail and brevity, provided $36,000, broken down as follows:

"For a beacon light on the Upper Jettee, Cape Fear river, three thousand five hundred dollars.

"For a beacon light on Campbell's island, same river, three thousand five hundred dollars.

"For a beacon light at Orton's point, same river, three thousand five hundred dollars.

"For a light-boat at the Horse Shoe, same river, between New Inlet and Price's Creek, ten thousand dollars.

"For two beacon lights placed in the best manner at Price's creek, six thousand dollars.

"For two light-houses placed in the best manner upon the west channel of the same river, and a keeper's house on Oak island, nine thousand dollars.

"For a buoy on the Western bar, and another at the rip off the point of Oak Island, same river, five hundred dollars."

It is difficult for anyone today to come up with a precise distinction between the words "beacon" and "lighthouse" as used in the congressional act of 1848. Even now the two are used interchangeably, and modern dictionaries list "lighthouse" as a primary definition of the word "beacon." Of the two, "beacon" is the older word, defined in an eighteenth-century dictionary as "a long pole set upon a rising ground, near the sea-coast, on which pitch-barrels are fastened ready to be fired, to give notice of invasions, prevent shipwrecks, &c." The word "lighthouse" was not even listed.

In 1848, when Congress authorized the construction of "beacon lights" at some locations along the lower Cape Fear and "lighthouses" at others, it appears that the difference was mainly in size and cost, with "beacon" being used generally to describe the smaller lighthouses. An examination of lower Cape Fear River navigation charts of the period reveals that the beacons authorized in August, 1848, were shown on the maps as lighthouses, with no distinction between them and the structures Congress actually described as "lighthouses." Regardless the name, within two years of the 1848 authorization all of the Cape Fear River lights with the exception of those on the Upper Jettee were completed and in service.

Probably the most important of these were the two lighthouses at Oak Island on the west side of the river mouth opposite Bald

Head. These were of special importance to vessels making their way down the river, for as the main channel approaches Oak Island from Southport it makes a sweeping curve to the east, and the proximity of shoals on either side called for precise navigation in order to avert disaster. The fifth auditor's lighthouse consultants reasoned that a single lighthouse placed on Oak Island would be inadequate and that two lights were needed, one behind the other, so that they could be lined up and used as range finders as the pilot brought his vessel into the broad curve in the channel.

The northernmost of the two lighthouses built on Oak Island, known as "the rear light," was the higher of the two, exhibiting a fixed white light thirty-seven feet above sea level, ten feet higher than its companion. Possibly as an economy move the light itself was "placed on a wooden tower, immediately over the center of the keeper's dwelling." You can take your pick of two different contemporary descriptions of the second tower, which was located south of the first one near the ocean beach. One early note lists it as being a brick tower "surrounded by sand hills"; another described it as "an open-frame frustum of a square pyramid resting on a tram railway, which allows of its being moved to the right or left, to suit the changes in the channel." One possible basis for the confusion could be that original plans called for the brick tower but when the time came to build it the movable frame structure was substituted; or there is even the possibility that the brick tower was located too close to the ocean and was washed away before being completed. Perhaps information will someday come to light that will explain the apparent contradiction.

Unfortunately, the twin lights at Oak Island were subsequently found to be poorly located to the extent that they did not serve the purpose of marking the range over the bar, "being so near each other that considerable deviation from the true course is necessary to make them appear to separate."

At about the same time in 1849 that the Oak Island lighthouses were placed in service, work was being completed on two others farther up the river at Campbell's Island and Orton's Point. The lights on both were twenty-nine feet above the water level, and both were built on elevated structures above the marsh, Orton's Point on the west side of the river and Campbell's Island in the middle, closer to Wilmington.

The rear beacon at Oak Island, illuminated in 1849, was rebuilt in 1879. The beacon stood thirty-seven feet above sea level. (Photo by Art Newton; from the library of David Stick.)

The two lighthouses at Price's Creek on the west side of the river above Southport were designed, as at Oak Island, to provide a range of lights that could be lined up by passing vessels as they navigated a bend in the river channel. The main structure was a wooden tower mounted on top of the keeper's dwelling, the focal plane of the light being twenty-two feet above ground level and thirty-five feet above mean high water. The second light was a circular brick structure, sixteen feet high, with the light twenty-five feet above the water.

Unfortunately, there are few known photographs of the pre-Civil War lighthouses in North Carolina, Price's Creek being an exception. A photograph in the State Archives, captioned "The Old Lighthouse, Price's Creek, Southport, N.C.," shows a large two-story brick structure, roughly square and measuring something like twenty-five feet across. At the time the picture was taken the building was obviously abandoned and in a state of deterioration, with the wooden light tower partially dismantled and leaning at a precarious angle. Two photographs remain of the other Price's Creek lighthouse, the first one showing a circular brick structure immediately adjacent to the river, with a window on the water side and a circular platform on top holding a skeleton framework for

"THE OLD LIGHTHOUSE," PRICE'S CREEK, SOUTHPORT, N. C.

The Price's Creek lighthouse, stationed on the west side of the Cape Fear River above Southport, was part of a chain of navigational aids for vessels following the channel to Wilmington. (Photo from the files of the Division of Archives and History.)

the light. A second photograph of the same structure shows the addition of another six or eight feet, and the circular platform has been replaced by a square one. This picture also reveals a gaping hole near ground level, apparently the result of a direct shell hit during Civil War fighting in the area.

With completion of the two lighthouses at Price's Creek, the bulk of the basic aids to navigation on the lower Cape Fear had been placed in operation during a period of only two years following authorization by Congress. The final major facility, the Horseshoe Shoal lightboat, was anchored on its station in 1851 at a strategic location near the middle of the river between New Inlet and Price's Creek. The light was forty-three feet above water level, and the vessel was also equipped with a fog horn and bell, which were sounded alternately at five-minute intervals during bad weather.

The final link in the chain of navigational aids on the Cape Fear, the Upper Jettee beacon just below Wilmington, for which $3,500 had been appropriated in 1848, was delayed when it was deter-

mined by an investigating team that the funds were "hardly sufficient for the intended object." As a result, there was a wait of
several years before additional money was appropriated to provide
two range lights on the approach to the port of Wilmington. These
were built on high banks on the east side of the river two and a half
to three miles below Wilmington and approximately 800 feet
apart. The larger one, with the light enclosed in an open
framework mounted atop the keeper's dwelling, was sixty-five feet
above sea level, while the light on the smaller one was listed as being forty-two feet above the water.

The Upper Jettee lights were made operational in 1855, just six
years before the outbreak of the Civil War, and for that brief period
of time vessels navigating the Cape Fear River could do so with
some assurance that they were not going to run aground on an unmarked shoal.

The second light at Price's Creek provided a range by which pilots could line up
the two lights as they steered through the river channel. (Photos from the files of the
Division of Archives and History.)

7

Filling in the Blind Spots

Fifth Auditor Stephen Pleasanton assumed responsibility for construction, maintenance, and operation of lighthouses throughout the United States in 1820, and for more than thirty years he directed the operation much as if he were king and the coastal areas his fiefdom. During his tenure twenty-three lighthouses and light vessels were installed in North Carolina waters, all but three of them in interior waters. The exceptions were the lighthouse built at Ocracoke in 1823, the Diamond Shoals lightship stationed intermittently off Cape Hatteras between 1824 and 1826, and the first Bodie Island lighthouse, placed in operation in 1848.

The Bodie Island project was initiated in 1837 when Pleasanton, spurred by Congress, appointed Lieutenant Napoleon L. Coste, commanding officer of the revenue cutter *Campbell*, to conduct a survey of the coast south of Chesapeake Bay to determine the need for additional lighthouses. One of his major recommendations was for the construction of a lighthouse on an isolated stretch of the North Carolina Outer Banks approximately thirty-five miles above Cape Hatteras. "More vessels are lost there than on any other part of our coast," Coste reported. "It is the eastern-most point of land on the coast of North Carolina, forming, in fact, a cape. It is my opinion, that, by the erection of a lighthouse on it, much property would be saved, and the navigation of the coast facilitated."

The specific area recommended by Coste was referred to in some reports as Bodie Island and in others as Pea Island. There should be little wonder over this uncertainty about place-names on the Outer Banks, for confusion exists even now when strangers hear, for example, that Pea Island is not really an island but instead is part of Hatteras Island; or that Bodie Island is not an island either, but in fact is the end of a peninsula attached to Nags Head, Kitty Hawk, and Virginia Beach.

Those who wonder how such misleading names can exist may be comforted by the knowledge that at one time in the past there was an island called Pea and another called Bodie (pronounced "body") and that there is a logical explanation, or at least one that is logical by Outer Banks standards, for the confusion. The reason, quite simply, is that throughout recorded history the topography of the Outer Banks has been subjected to a continuing process of change as new inlets opened and old ones closed. No single spot on the coast has been more affected by such changes than the area above Chicamacomico where Lieutenant Coste proposed the erection of a major lighthouse, for there have been at least six different inlets there in a distance of less than fifteen miles. Only one of these, Oregon Inlet, remains today, however; and, since it cut right through the middle of the old Bodie Island when it opened in an 1846 hurricane, a person could further complicate the matter by stating, and correctly so, that the opening of Oregon Inlet actually created two Bodie Islands, though neither one exists as an island today.

Even though Congress appropriated $5,000 for the proposed lighthouse there was so much disagreement as to the specific location that it was five years before a deed for the land was secured from a man named John Midgett. Further delays were encountered in the process of planning a suitable lighthouse for the site, partly because one inspector claimed there was a good base of hard clay, another said the material was sand, and residents of the area claimed it was nothing but a mixture of sand and mud, which eventually proved to be the case. The result was that the lighthouse still had not been built when Oregon Inlet opened across the banks a short distance north of the site, though it had then been nine years since Lieutenant Coste had made his initial proposal.

Finally, in the summer of 1847 bids were advertised and a contract awarded to Francis A. Gibbons of Baltimore for construction of a circular brick structure, fifty-four feet tall, with a diameter of seventeen feet at its base and twelve and one-half feet at the top. The ungainly appearing structure was later described as "looking much like an upside down ice cream cone with about one-third of its small end cut off."

The cost of the brick lighthouse plus a five-room frame dwelling house for the keeper, a 2,000-gallon brick cistern, and two outbuildings was $8,750, with another $2,350 paid Winslow Lewis for installing a lantern, ten feet in diameter, equipped with a revolving light. The exact date on which the first Bodie Island lighthouse was placed in operation is not known, though it was sometime in the spring of 1848. A man named Samuel Tilles (or Tillett) was appointed as keeper at an annual salary of $400.

There were problems from the outset. To begin with, the original keeper was dismissed and a new one, John B. Etheridge, appointed in his place only a year or so after the lighthouse was completed. Shortly thereafter it was discovered that one side of the base of the tower was a foot lower than the other with the result that it "canted to eastward," certainly not as noticeable a problem as with the famed Leaning Tower of Pisa, but a matter for concern nonetheless.

There were additional problems with the lighting apparatus, which consisted of fourteen lamps equipped with individual parabolic reflectors. The lamps and reflectors rested on a chandelier that was rotated by means of a falling weight attached to a system of gears and flywheels to control the speed of the rotation. It was this rotation of the chandelier that produced a flashing effect, but the intricate mechanism, called a clockwork system, was soon discovered to be operating erratically, most likely as a result of the tower being out of center.

The first Bodie Island lighthouse was the last major light erected in North Carolina under the direction of Fifth Auditor Stephen Pleasanton, for his reign was coming to an end. He had been the keeper of America's lights and the guardian of its shores for nearly a third of a century, but despite a tremendous increase in the number of lighthouses and light vessels during that period there had been growing dissatisfaction with the quality of the new lights and the overall management of the lighthouse service. The final blow to Pleasanton came in a single sentence near the end of a lengthy lighthouse authorization bill dated March 3, 1851, in which the secretary of the treasury was instructed "to cause a board to be convened . . . to inquire into the condition of the lighthouse establishment of the United States, and make a general detailed report and programme to guide legislation in extending and improving our present system of construction, illumination, inspection, and superintendence."

This temporary lighthouse board was composed of two high ranking naval officers, two officers of the Army Corps of Engineers, and the superintendent of the United States Coast Survey, with naval Captain W. B. Shubrick serving as chairman and a naval lieutenant as secretary. Throughout the spring, summer, and fall of 1851 the members of this board went about the task of investigating all aspects of the subject, with individual members making personal inspections of lighthouses and light vessels throughout this country and in Europe as well.

The detailed report of the board, presented to the secretary of the treasury in January, 1852, contained more than 700 pages plus numerous charts and illustrations and was a stinging critique of the nation's lights, of the management of the lighthouse establishment, and even of the methods employed by Congress in providing funds for the service. "The light-houses, light-vessels, beacons and buoys and their accessories in the United States, are not as efficient as the interests of commerce, navigation and humanity demand," the report stated. "They do not compare favorably with similar aids to navigation in Europe," it continued, noting that the lighthouse establishments in Great Britain and France were operated more economically.

The board listed two primary reasons for these deficiencies. First, it reported, "there has never been an efficient systematic plan of construction, illumination, inspection, and superintendence of lights, &c., in the United States." Then, pointing a finger at the elected representatives in Washington, the report concluded that "lights and other aids to navigation are provided, as a general rule, through the action of Congress upon the petitions emanating from persons having a local interest, or from boards of pilots, insurance offices, chambers of commerce, &c."

In a seven-page list of specific shortcomings the board found that the illuminating apparatus used throughout the United States was of a type "nearly obsolete throughout all maritime countries," while the lights, both ashore and afloat, were "not sufficiently well distinguished" either by day or by night. The board reported that there was "no system" in the management of the lighthouse establishment; that there was not, "in useful effect, a single first-class light on the coast of the United States"; that "the modern lighthouse towers are inferior in point of materials and workmanship to the older ones visited by the board"; that "the floating lights of the United States are comparatively useless," being defective "in size, model and moorings"; and that great confusion existed because changes in the lights were "constantly taking place without any official notice being given" to mariners. Of special interest to North Carolinians was the board's comment that the lights along the southern coast "are comparatively useless to the mariner for want of sufficient power or range."

To correct these deficiencies the board recommended a complete reorganization of the lighthouse operations and specifically the establishment of a Light House Board, "to be charged by law with the entire management of the light-house establishment in the United States." Among the specific recommendations was one that "no light-house keeper be appointed who cannot read and write, and is not in other respects competent to the faithful discharge of the duties."

Present-day students of government could do well to study the sequence of events leading up to and then following the report of this special board, for it is a classic example of the legislative process at work. It began with the acknowledgment by Congress in March, 1851, that something was wrong with the country's lighthouse operations and instructions to the treasury secretary to appoint a high-level board to make a thorough study of the problem. Then came the systematic investigation conducted by the board that culminated in its 700-page detailed report, quickly followed by hearings before congressional committees, the drafting of appropriate legislation, and finally the passage of a new law creating a nine-member Light House Board vested with full responsibility and authority for putting the lighthouse establishment in order. All of this took place in a period of less than twenty months between the call for an investigation in March, 1851, and the act creating the Light House Board in October, 1852.

Two additional lights were placed on the North Carolina coast in 1852 and 1853, the concluding efforts of the Pleasanton administration. Both were in the vicinity of Ocracoke Inlet, a thirty-nine-foot-high lighthouse on Beacon Island and a new lightboat with two lights (one thirty-nine feet and the other twenty-eight feet above water level) in the ever changing Ocracoke channel. By 1857, however, both were found to be "useless," and consideration was being given to abandoning them.

The North Carolina coast was an early beneficiary of the establishment of the new Light House Board. In 1854 a first-order lightship equipped with two lights forty feet above the water level was put in service off Cape Fear to mark the dangerous Frying Pan Shoals. A year later two small lighthouses were constructed on Bogue Banks to provide for the first time adequate navigational aids into the major harbor at Beaufort Inlet (formerly Old Topsail Inlet). The larger of the structures, equipped with "a fourth order lens, fifty feet above the sea, surmounting a tower made of excellent bricks," was erected on the eastern point of Bogue Banks. It provided guidance through Beaufort Inlet by ranging with a smaller light located approximately half a mile away. The smaller light stood "thirty feet above the sea, supported by a wooden frame."

The final new North Carolina project undertaken by the Light House Board in the late 1850s was the establishment of a twenty-five-foot-high beacon "near the point of Cape Hatteras," a needed supplement to the Cape Hatteras lighthouse that was actually located something like a mile north of the cape itself and a considerable distance inland.

With these projects the new Light House Board had completed the task of filling in the blind spots both on the coast and the inland waters of North Carolina; but much work remained if the board was to fulfill its responsibilities in bringing about a complete overhaul of the country's lighthouse establishment.

8

The Light House Board Takes Over

Complaints about the quality of the lights on the North Carolina coast continued after the new Light House Board took over in the 1850s, and in the case of much-maligned Cape Hatteras they seemed even more vociferous than ever. Cape Hatteras lighthouse was described by one coastal captain as "a disgrace to our country." Another said it was "the most important light in the world," and that on his first nine trips down the coast he "never saw Hatteras light at all, though frequently passing in sight of the breakers; and when I did see it, I could not tell it from a steamer's light, excepting that the steamer's lights are much brighter." Still another complained that Cape Hatteras and the other so-called major lights on the coast "if not improved, had better be dispensed with, as the navigator is apt to run ashore looking for them."

One of the unique problems at Cape Hatteras was that a blanket of haze frequently formed over nearby Diamond Shoals and the cape itself. This haze has been attributed partly to the collision just offshore of the warm waters of the Gulf Stream and the colder currents coursing down from the north and partly to the constant upheaval of the waves, which always seem to be in a state of turbulence over the shoals. Sometimes this blanket of haze hugs the land, but often it seems to form a shroud floating above the cape, eighty, ninety, or even a hundred feet or more above the sandy land. In a later time the keeper of the Cape Hatteras Lifesaving Station frequently referred to conditions as being "smoky" when the blanket of haze was hanging low over the shoals.

A frequent complaint about the original Cape Hatteras lighthouse, with its light shining at an elevation of ninety feet or so above the water level, was that it was too high to be seen below the mantle of haze and too low to be seen above it. At one time during the Pleasanton administration there was even consideration of lowering the light so it would shine below the mist, but it was determined that this would preclude the light being seen at a sufficient distance to serve as a warning for vessels approaching Diamond Shoals. The idea was rejected.

The Light House Board took the opposite approach and in March, 1853, received congressional approval to spend $15,000 to elevate the Cape Hatteras tower to a height of 150 feet. Brick was the basic material used in elevating the tower, and in order to provide it with distinctive coloring by day the bottom seventy feet of the refurbished lighthouse was whitewashed and the upper eighty feet was painted red.

The expensive job of elevating the tower at Cape Hatteras was only the first step in providing this most dangerous of coastal locations with an adequate lighthouse facility, for it was equally important to make major improvements in the light itself. Until comparatively modern times when electricity came into use in lighthouses, there were always two basic elements to the light. The first was a flame, generated initially by burning wood, then coal, then candles, and finally various kinds of oil. The second was a lens and/or reflectors, which served both to shield the flame and to magnify the light. In 1812 the United States had purchased the patent for a system of lamps and reflectors developed by a ship captain named Winslow Lewis. He in turn had adapted the system from similar equipment in use in Europe. It consisted of a lamp with a hollow circular wick, a type originally introduced in France in 1781 by a man named Ami Argand, and a parabolic reflector set behind each lamp. By 1815 Lewis had installed his system in all forty-nine of the nation's lighthouses and continued to do so throughout most of the tenure of the fifth auditor.

The inefficiency of the Lewis lighting system was frequently listed as a primary reason for the poor quality of lighthouses in the United States. When it came time to provide a light for the newly elevated tower at Cape Hatteras, the Light House Board ordered the installation of a first-order lens of a unique design that had been developed by a French physicist named Augustin Fresnel.

An excellent and concise description of the Fresnel lens appears in Francis Ross Holland, Jr.'s, *America's Lighthouses* and is reprinted here with his permission:

> Fresnel's lens [Holland writes] resembled a gigantic beehive that surrounded a single lamp. Prisms at the top and bottom refracted, or bent, the light so that it came from the lens in a narrow sheet. At the same time, the light was intensified at the center of the lens by a powerful magnifying glass. The result of this refraction and magnification was a bright, narrow sheet of concentrated light emitting from the lighthouse.
>
> Fresnel devised seven orders, or sizes, of lens, depending upon the power of the light needed. The first-order lens was the largest and gave the most powerful light and would be used as a seacoast light. The smallest was a sixth-order lens for use in harbors.

Even as work was going forward on refurbishing the Cape Hatteras lighthouse and installing a first-order Fresnel lens, a number of prominent citizens of Edenton, Elizabeth City, and other communities in the Albemarle area of North Carolina were petitioning the government to build a lighthouse at Roanoke Marshes, the same area in which a lighthouse had been built and then abandoned in the early 1830s on the disputed Van Pelt property. In his letter of transmittal to the Light House Board the local collector and superintendent of lights, L. D. Starke, pointed out that the passage through Roanoke Marshes "is only some three or four hundred yards in width; that there are no high lands or trees by which to direct the course of ships; that there is no light in the vicinity; that the sound is very much exposed and dangerous; and that it is always difficult, and frequently impossible, to effect an entrance into the narrow passage alluded to, at night or in thick, foggy weather."

During the 1850s attempts were made to renovate the first Cape Lookout lighthouse, erected in 1812, but federal officials eventually decided to replace the outmoded ninety-six-foot tower with a 150-foot one. Shown here is the Cape Lookout light station 1893. (Photo courtesy of the Mariners' Museum, Newport News, Virginia.)

The Cape Lookout lighthouse, completed in 1859, became the model for all the lighthouses subsequently constructed along the Outer Banks. (Photo from the files of the U.S. Coast Guard.)

The board responded favorably and construction was begun in 1857 on a structure resting on a foundation of "seven wood piles covered with cast iron . . . screwed into the ground several feet." Exhibiting a light thirty-three feet above the water level, this was the first of the so-called "screw pile lighthouses" in North Carolina. Subsequently, a similar structure was erected at Wade's Point near the mouth of the Pasquotank River to replace the lightboat there.

Meanwhile, the problems at the relatively new Bodie Island lighthouse had become so serious that the Light House Board determined it was not feasible to try to repair the structure, and in 1858 Congress appropriated $25,000 for a new lighthouse at the site. Erected close to the original tower and south of Oregon Inlet, this second Bodie Island lighthouse was a tall, graceful brick structure exhibiting its light approximately ninety feet above sea level. Painted white and equipped with a revolving third-order Fresnel lens that flashed every ninety seconds, the light was designed to be seen at a distance of fifteen miles.

One more major coastal job remained in North Carolina, for the old Cape Lookout lighthouse, built in 1812, had outlived its effectiveness. Apparently the tower itself, ninety-six feet high and built on a small sand dune so that the light was 104 feet above sea level, had remained in good condition, for the first step taken by the Light House Board was to replace the old lighting mechanism with a first-order Fresnel lens. This measure proved unsatisfactory, however; and, when it was determined that it would not be practical to elevate the old tower, as had been done at Cape Hatteras, work went forward on construction of an entirely new Cape Lookout lighthouse.

The new tower, 150 feet above ground level and exhibiting its light 156 feet above the surrounding waters, was begun in 1857 and completed in 1859. A simple yet graceful circular red brick structure, the new Cape Lookout lighthouse was almost universally admired, both for its appearance and its effectiveness, and though no one was aware of it at the time the Cape Lookout tower was to become the prototype for all of the lighthouses subsequently erected along the Outer Banks.

Thus, on the eve of the Civil War all of the North Carolina coast with the exception of the extreme northern part was provided with substantial lighthouses equipped with the most modern Fresnel lenses, while most of the interior channels, rivers, and inlets were marked with smaller lighthouses or with lightboats.

9

The Lights Go Out

The sparsely populated and largely isolated coast of North Carolina assumed a position of special importance as civil war erupted in America, for the coast was North Carolina's first line of defense against enemy attack. At the same time its inlets were the funnels through which contact could be maintained with allies and much-needed supplies could be brought into the state. Defense of these vital inlets was a first order of business and the task of building forts to protect them was pushed forward with vigor, first by the state and then by the newly formed Confederate government.

On the northern coast the two inlets that had been opened through the Outer Banks during the course of the same storm in September, 1846, had already begun to assume major importance by 1861. The more southern of the two, Hatteras Inlet, though in existence for only fifteen years, had already replaced Ocracoke Inlet as the largest, deepest, and most stable inlet connecting Pamlico Sound and its tributaries with the sea. The other one, Oregon Inlet, though relatively shallow and thus undependable, was nonetheless a direct link with the north end of Pamlico Sound and the trading centers of the Albemarle region.

A small fortification, Fort Oregon, was built on the south side of Oregon Inlet between the inlet and the new Bodie Island lighthouse. Two much more extensive ones, Fort Hatteras and Fort Clark, were placed on the Cape Hatteras side of Hatteras Inlet, since it was assumed any Federal fleet attempting to enter the sounds would have to come that way. Just to be on the safe side, however, another small fort was constructed on Beacon Island, inside Ocracoke Inlet and immediately adjacent to the lighthouse that had been built there in 1853. Appropriately it was named Fort Ocracoke.

All of these efforts were designed to prevent the enemy from gaining access to the sounds, but someone involved in the planning of the state's defenses was realist enough to understand that these coastal defenses might not be able to hold back a determined Federal assault, so consideration was given to a second line of defense. The object this time was to prevent an invading fleet from moving from Pamlico Sound past Roanoke Island to Albemarle Sound and its tributaries, which meant that the narrow channel through Croatan Sound was the key spot to be defended.

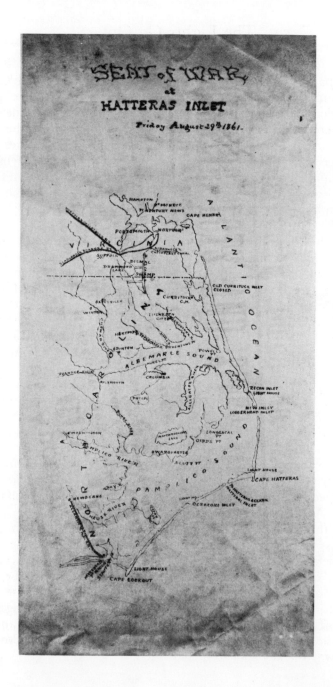

Because the Roanoke Marshes at the south end of Croatan Sound provided such a poor foundation for the erection of fortifications, the major defensive line was planned for the north end of the sound. A line of obstructions, consisting of sunken vessels and cutoff pilings— *chevaux de frise*—was placed across the north end of the sound from Roanoke Island to the mainland, leaving only a small opening at the channel. Two forts were built on the high land on the Roanoke Island side, but the prospect of trying to build conventional fortifications on the marshy mainland shores west of the sound proved so formidable that it was decided to sink an old vessel there and mount guns on her deck, a quick and ingenious means of providing a much-needed fort. Thus, the defenders would be able, in theory at least, to destroy any enemy vessels unfortunate enough to become bottled up below the line of obstructions.

The initial attack came in late August, 1861, just three months after North Carolina seceded from the Union, when a formidable fleet moved against Hatteras Inlet. After two days of heavy fighting, both afloat and ashore, Fort Hatteras and Fort Clark fell to the Union forces.

In late September, Fort Ocracoke was captured after a heavy bombardment, during the course of which the Beacon Island lighthouse was rendered inoperable. Attention was then directed to Oregon Inlet, but before the Federal forces could capture Fort Oregon the Confederate defenders, fearing that all of Hatteras Island would soon be in enemy hands, blew up the three-year-old lighthouse on Bodie Island. Retreating down the banks in disorder, past Chicamacomico and Kinnakeet in what was later referred to as "The Chicamacomico Races," the defenders made a hurried effort to render the Cape Hatteras lighthouse inoperable but succeeded only in removing the lantern and lens.

The battle of Roanoke Island, which followed in early 1862, was a short-lived affair. The Union forces under command of General Ambrose E. Burnside—he with such a distinctive growth of hair on the sides of his face that the style immediately became known as "Side-Burns"—refused to be drawn into the trap at the north end of Croatan Sound. Instead he landed his 7,000 men under cover of

Facing page: During the Union attack on Fort Hatteras in 1861, Joseph Isaacs drew this map of the "seat of war" in his diary. (The diary is in the possession of the Division of Archives and History.)

darkness at Ashby's Harbor near the center of the island. The follow-ing morning Burnside's troops quickly subdued the interior fortifica-tions and were in complete control of the island in time for a late luncheon. In the course of the mop-up operations that followed, the entire Albemarle section of North Carolina passed into Federal con-trol.

With the northern coast secure Federal attention was next di-rected toward the Cape Lookout-Bogue Banks-Beaufort area and the Cape Fear. At Beaufort Inlet a major fortification, dating from 1834 and named Fort Macon, was attacked and captured in April, 1862, though not before all of the lighthouses and beacons on Bogue Banks had been destroyed by Confederate defenders. At Cape Lookout, the new 150-foot-high Cape Lookout lighthouse had been damaged only slightly by the retreating forces, though the lens had been rendered inoperative, resulting in yet another major navigational aid being extinguished.

The defenders did better, much better, in the Cape Fear area, aided at least in part by a distinctive natural process that occurs in areas where the waters from major rivers flow through sandy beaches to the sea. Rivers such as the Cape Fear serve as funnels through which huge quantities of rainwater, gathering initially in in-numerable tributaries fanning out over the mountains and Pied-mont, are transported to the ocean. The flow of water varies, with the highest volume normally occurring after heavy spring rains and the smallest during the dry months, the result being a process of con-stant change in the depth, width, and location of the channels near the ocean as the flow of water fluctuates from trickle to torrent and back again. Sometimes during periods of exceptionally high flow completely new channels are opened and quickly scoured out enough to accommodate the normal volume of water. At such times the older channels and inlets, deprived of the flow of moving water that keeps them open, are rendered useless for maritime traffic.

Such a change took place in the early part of the nineteenth cen-tury when New Inlet opened some eight miles up the shore from Bald Head and the established mouth of the Cape Fear River. Because of the importance of keeping open the port of Wilmington, major Con-federate defensive works were constructed on the coast on the east side of New Inlet. These defenses, known as Fort Fisher, were suf-ficiently formidable to discourage Union attacks until late in the war, and with other major ports in Union hands, both to the north and to the south, the Cape Fear became a lifeline through which essential supplies could be fed to the northern areas of the Confederacy.

Not until the second battle of Fort Fisher in January, 1865, did control of Fort Fisher and thus of the Cape Fear River pass into Union hands. Before surrendering, however, the defenders destroyed or rendered inoperative most of the lights in the area, including the Bald Head and Federal Point lighthouses on the coast, and the Horseshoe Shoal lightboat and the smaller lighthouses at Price's Creek, Orton's Point, Campbell's Island, and the Upper Jettee on the Cape Fear River.

By that time practically all of the remaining light stations had fallen into Union hands, though in most cases the lights were extinguished by Confederate forces before being captured. Those at Ocracoke, Roanoke Marshes, Pamlico Point, and the Northwest Point of Royal Shoal were repaired and again placed in service by Federal forces. At Wade's Point and Croatan the superstructures had been set afire and so badly damaged that they could not be repaired until after the end of the war, and the lightboat at Brant Island Shoal, commandeered by North Carolina troops early in the conflict but recaptured by the Federal troops who took Hatteras Inlet, "was subsequently sunk by accident at that inlet." She was later raised and placed back on her station after extensive repairs.

In retrospect, what a strange sequence of events. The residents of North Carolina had argued, scrounged, and begged for lighthouses from their own government throughout the colonial period, but without results. Then the federal government stepped in and provided most of the North Carolina coast and its major inlets and interior channels with the protection of lighthouses and light vessels, only to have North Carolinians destroy them in one more improbable act in that improbable conflict between North and South.

10

Screw-Pile Lighthouses

During the period immediately prior to the Civil War the Light House Board had conducted detailed studies of lighthouse operations in foreign countries. A noticeable result was the adoption of many of the best features employed in the construction of the European lighthouses, of which a prime example was the decision to equip all American lighthouses with the superior Fresnel lens systems.

Another important and far-reaching step taken by the board was the adoption of a policy to replace all light vessels in interior waters with screw-pile lighthouses. This simple yet almost revolutionary concept, developed specifically as a means of building and retaining lighthouses in relatively shallow water where there was continual exposure to strong tides and heavy winds, was the invention of an Englishman, Alexander Mitchell. The first of his screw-pile lighthouses was built in the late 1830s.

A concise description of Mitchell's unique design is given by lighthouse authority Francis Ross Holland, Jr., in his impressive book, *America's Lighthouses*: "The screw-pile lighthouse is similar to other pile-type lighthouses except that the end of each pile is equipped with a broad-bladed screw. The screw is twisted into a sand or coral bottom much as one twists a screw into a piece of wood. Not only is the screw a means for getting the pile into the ocean bottom, but its three-foot blade provides additional bearing surface."

The conventional design for early screw-pile lighthouses was a hexagonal multistoried structure—a sort of six-sided layer-cake design with gingerbread adornments and decorations. Since the building was mounted on top of the foundation of screw-piles, usually six or eight in number with the ground floor elevated ten or twelve feet above the water, it tended to remind the uninitiated viewer of a huge spiderlike creature with its single eye giving off a piercing light.

Married men appointed as keepers of the isolated screw-pile lighthouses usually kept their families on board, so that the structure served not only as home and workshop, but as school, church, and playground as well. Almost invariably the first floor was surrounded on all six sides by a covered porch, with a railing on the

The screw-pile lighthouse at Harbor Island was built in 1867. These lighthouses replaced light vessels in North Carolina's interior waters after the Civil War. (Photo from the files of the North Carolina Museum of Natural History.)

outer edge. Normally a door was located on one side, pairs of windows on a couple more, and a single window or door on others. This main floor housed the keeper and his family—a home at sea complete with kitchen, dining and living areas, plus one or two bedrooms and office space.

Centered on top of the main structure was a small low-ceilinged room, most often with windows on three sides through which the keeper could take observations without having to go outside. Stairs led from this little room to the lantern above, which was surrounded by a widow's-walk-type gallery and a railing, both hexagonal in design. An unusual feature of most screw-pile lighthouses was a small tunnellike passageway—a sort of miniature covered bridge—mounted on top of the main roof to provide the keeper with protected access to the fog bell when he had to ring it manually in bad weather. In later years the hexagonal design was supplanted by a more conventional square structure making possible the addition of a large upper room or attic. Steps usually led down toward the water from the interior of the first-floor house, providing protected access to small boats, which when not in use were hung from davits attached to the main porch.

The first North Carolina screw-pile lighthouses were built between 1856 and 1860 at Wade's Point, Croatan, and the Northwest Point of Royal Shoal to replace lightboats, and at Roanoke Marshes. Following the war, the burned-out structures at Wade's Point and Croatan were rebuilt and relighted, and more new screw-piles were added rapidly, beginning with one at Federal Point in 1866. The following year four more were built: at Long Shoal, Harbor Island, the Southwest Point of Royal Shoal, and the mouth of the Roanoke River. Screw-piles were added at Horseshoe Shoal in 1868, at the mouth of the Neuse River in 1869, and finally at Brant Island Shoal in 1877. Other screw-pile lighthouses were established at new locations, beginning with one at the mouth of the North River in 1868; at Oliver's Reef near Hatteras Inlet in

Among the first screw-pile lighthouses built in North Carolina between 1856 and 1860 was the one at Roanoke Marshes. It was not decommissioned until 1955. (Photo from the files of the U.S. Coast Guard.)

1874; Laurel Point in Albemarle Sound in 1880; and Gull Shoal on the west side of Pamlico Sound in 1891.

The lighthouses on the Cape Fear River south of Wilmington, extinguished during the war, were not replaced, except for the screw-pile at Federal Point near New Inlet and the small lighthouses on Oak Island near the mouth of the main river. Temporary day markers were erected to take the place of the other lights on the Cape Fear, and in the 1880s a series of fourteen unattended range beacons, for the most part consisting of lanterns mounted on top of pilings, were installed to aid mariners navigating the lower reaches of the river.

Other range markers were installed to mark less traveled channels in the more northern waters, beginning with four in Currituck Sound, two on the North River, and two others at Edenton Bay, including one mounted on shore in the top of a tree.

The screw-pile lighthouses, which became a distinctive feature of North Carolina's inland waters in the period just before and after the Civil War, continued in service in some instances for nearly a century. They offered finally the degree of reliability in navigational aids so long sought by those using our vast sound and river waterways.

After the Civil War the Light House Board gave top priority to the construction of a new lighthouse at Cape Hatteras. The lighthouse, completed in 1870, is pictured here in 1954. (Photo by Aycock Brown; from the library of David Stick.)

11

Majestic Coastal Towers

One area of primary concern in North Carolina still remained for consideration by the Light House Board following the Civil War. This was the northern coast, a stretch of the Outer Banks extending from Cape Hatteras northward to the Virginia line, and beyond that to Cape Henry at the entrance to Chesapeake Bay. As a result of the destruction of the second Bodie Island lighthouse during the early part of the war, there were no navigational aids of any kind between Cape Hatteras and Cape Henry, a distance of 120 miles.

The plan first considered was to build one new lighthouse at Pea Island, near the site of the old Bodie Island light station, and another at Paul Gamiel's Hill north of Kitty Hawk. But this plan still left an exceptionally long void south of Cape Henry. So consideration was given to erecting three new lighthouses equally spaced at intervals of approximately thirty miles from Cape Henry to Cape Hatteras. The final decision, however, was to build an entirely new lighthouse at Cape Hatteras, taller than any ever built in America, and two more at forty-mile intervals between there and Cape Henry. The objective, in planning these structures and their lights, was to enable coastal shipping to pick up sight of the light ahead before losing sight of the one astern. By day this called for tall distinctly marked towers and by night the latest and most powerful lighting apparatus available.

Priority was given to the new Cape Hatteras lighthouse, and in March, 1867, Congress appropriated $75,000 for the project. The new tower was to be patterned after the highly regarded Cape Lookout lighthouse of 1859 and to be in fact its twin sister, except that at 180 feet it was considerably higher and thus of necessity more ponderous from foundation to lantern.

From the outset the Light House Board emphasized that "quality is a much greater object than price," both in materials and in workmanship, a marked departure from the earlier approach of the penny-pinching fifth auditor. "In a tower so expensive and exposed as the new one proposed for Cape Hatteras," the board stated, "it is desirable to take every measure to secure the very best materials." Lest the point should be missed, it was reaffirmed in a directive to the district engineer, which read in part:

"It is the desire of the Board that this structure shall be of as durable a character as the nature of the materials . . . will admit."

More than a hundred years later visitors to the imposing tower sitting out there on the headlands of the cape can attest to its durability, even as they speculate on how it was possible for so massive a structure to be built in such an isolated spot with century-old technology. It was not an easy task.

The first problem that had to be solved was how to get materials to the job, and even by today's standards the logistics seem impressive. All shipments had to be made on small shallow-draft steamers and sailing vessels through the open sounds, but such craft, loaded with granite or brick or other materials, drew too much water to reach the sound shore back of the cape. It was therefore necessary to transfer all cargo to lighters in the open sound. Specifically designed scows, two with decks and a third one open, were built for the purpose. But the scows could not get all the way to shore either, so a long wharf had to be built out into the sound. The mile and a quarter from the wharf to the site of the proposed lighthouse consisted of mucky marsh and soft sand. This problem, in turn, was solved by building a tram railway from the end of the wharf to the construction site.

Instead of contracting with a private firm for the project, the Light House Board took on the job with its own crew, hired a foreman, and employed day labor, all under the general direction of a district engineer. The foreman selected for the Cape Hatteras project was Dexter Stetson, a man ingenious enough to figure out new ways of getting things done and capable of doing them. A contract was awarded to Nicholas M. Smith of Baltimore for one million "prime dark red brick" at a cost of $12.35 per thousand. Stone for the foundation and steps was to be supplied by Beattie, Dawson & Co.; metal and the oil tanks by Bartlett, Robbins & Co.; and all of it was to be delivered to the cape by the firm of Lennox and Burgess of Philadelphia.

Dexter Stetson's working party was on the job in early November, 1868. Construction began on quarters and a messroom for the crew, a blacksmith shop, two derricks, and storage buildings for cement and other perishable materials, as well as the wharf, tram railway, and scows.

One of the vessels transporting materials and supplies to the job,

The Cape Hatteras lighthouse, shown here in 1893, required complex logistics and the engineering genius of Dexter Stetson to rise from the soft sands of the Outer Banks' low beaches. (Photo from the files of the U.S. Coast Guard.)

the schooner *Ida Nicholson*, was reported to have sunk in a gale within site of the cape, losing more than 100,000 bricks in the process; and another, the *J. Parker*, went ashore at Nags Head with the loss of an additional 50,000 bricks. Still another loss occurred when one of the lighters, loaded with granite for the foundation, capsized in the sound.

Because the lighthouse was to be constructed on a relatively low beach covered with soft sand, there was special concern about the foundation. Original plans had called for driving heavy pilings into the sand as support for the huge blocks of granite that were to serve as a base for the tower, but Stetson found that he could drive a sounding rod only nine feet into the sand. He then discovered one of those contradictions of nature that coastal residents tend to take for granted. The very same sand that is so dry and soft near the surface that a man's foot will sink to a depth of an inch or two with every step is almost invariably damp and compact only a couple of feet down. It thus forms an exceptionally sturdy foundation capable of supporting tremendous weight.

Accordingly, Stetson proceeded to excavate a wide hole six feet deep. Finding that he could drive the pilings only six more feet below that level as a result of "the sand being very hard and compact," he devised an entirely different method of supporting the structure. Because his six-foot hole had rapidly filled with water, he took advantage of another phenomenon of nature: the resistance of certain types of wood to rotting so long as it is totally submerged in water and thus not exposed to the air. By building a cofferdam around his huge hole in the sand, he was able to keep the hole free of water with the use of "powerful steam engines." He then laid a course of six-by-twelve-inch yellow pine timbers in the bottom of the hole and placed a second course of six-by-twelves crossway on top of the first layer. Using the timbers as a base, he then "laid a massive octagonal foundation, composed of large blocks of granite laid in cement mortar, as rubble masonry, the interstices being filled with smaller stone of the same kind." When this was done he turned off the steam engines and let the water seep back into the hole, covering the pine timbers.

From the ground level four more octagonal courses of cut granite were added, each narrower than the preceding one, thus giving the outward appearance of huge stone steps surrounding the exposed foundation. Above this foundation for a height of approximately ten feet cut granite was laid at each corner with solid brick between, thus providing a base sufficient to support the weight of the massive circular brick tower that was to rise above it.

As the crew of masons continued to lay course after course of brick, gradually reducing the diameter of the tower as they worked skyward, steel stairways were installed. When at last the structure was completed, the Light House Board shipped down a first-order flashing lens of the most modern design with a lampist named George J. Crossman to install it properly.

When the new light was exhibited for the first time in the fall of 1870 (there is confusion about the exact date, though it was sometime between September 17 and December 20), North Carolina could boast of having "the most imposing and substantial brick lighthouse on this continent, if not in the world."

Shortly thereafter the lens was removed from the old lighthouse and plans readied for its destruction. On February 16, 1871, the district engineer reported that "three mines were fired almost

Dexter Stetson also constructed the new Bodie Island light station in 1872. The 150-foot tower is visible from a distance of nineteen miles. (Photo from the files of the U.S. Coast Guard.)

simultaneously blowing out a large wedge on the side toward the beach & this old land mark was spread out on the beach a mass of ruins.''

With the subsequent completion of a new home for the lighthouse keepers—there were three of them assigned to Cape Hatteras—the job there was done, and the equipment, including the tram railway, the storage buildings, and the scows, was moved up the beach where construction was about to begin on the new Bodie Island lighthouse.

The Bodie Island site, fifteen acres, was purchased at a cost of $150 from John B. Etheridge, a former keeper of the pre-Civil War lighthouse there. The new location was north of Oregon Inlet, which had already migrated so far to the south that it was within 400 yards of the site of the old light.

Dexter Stetson was again in charge of construction, and he used the same technique he had employed at Cape Hatteras in providing a foundation for the new Bodie Island tower—two courses of six-by-twelve timbers laid at right angles at the bottom of a seven-foot pit some four feet below the water level, with

In 1873 the Light House Board decreed that Cape Hatteras lighthouse should be painted in spiral bands, Cape Lookout in checkers, and Bodie Island in horizontal bands. (Cape Hatteras photo by Aycock Brown, from the library of David Stick; Cape Lookout and Bodie Island photos from the files of the U.S. Coast Guard.)

eighteen-inch-thick granite blocks on top of the timber and the base and light tower above that.

The Bodie Island lighthouse was almost identical in design to the older lighthouse at Cape Lookout, with its first-order lens sending out a flashing beam from a focal point 150 feet high. It was first lighted on October 1, 1872.

Still remaining was the eighty-mile void between Bodie Island and Cape Henry, and a decision was made to build a new first-order lighthouse almost exactly half way between the two on Currituck Beach at the community known as Corolla. The necessary land was purchased from Edmund C. Lindsey, and once again the older Cape Lookout design served as the prototype. Work was pushed forward on construction of a red brick tower with a focal plane of 150 feet and a substantial building to house the keepers. The new Currituck Beach lighthouse was illuminated for the first time on December 1, 1875.

With four lighthouses in the same coastal area almost identical in appearance, the Light House Board realized that mariners would be confused unless they could come up with distinctive markings for each. Accordingly, under date of April 17, 1873, the board issued a notice to mariners announcing changes that would make the towers "more readily distinguishable in the daytime":

"*Cape Hatteras* tower will be painted in *spiral bands*, alternately black and white.

To distinguish the Currituck Beach lighthouse, shown here in 1893, from others on the Outer Banks, the tower retained its natural red brick color. (Photo from the files of the U.S. Coast Guard.)

"*Cape Lookout* tower will be *checkered*, the checkers being painted alternately black and white.

"*Body's Island* tower is now painted in black and white *horizontal bands.*"

This still left the Currituck Beach lighthouse that was then in the planning stages, but the problem was solved subsequently when it was decided not to paint Currituck Beach at all, but to leave it a natural red brick color instead.

At the time no one seemed to realize that the so-called "checkers" at Cape Lookout actually produced a diamond-shaped pattern that would have been a much more appropriate design for Cape Hatteras and Diamond Shoals than for Cape Lookout and Lookout Shoals. But the often repeated story that the contractor made a mistake is in error.

In a period of only five years from 1870 to 1875 the Light House Board had completed major coastal lighthouses at Cape Hatteras, Bodie Island, and Currituck Beach and had given the prototype at Cape Lookout a distinctive paint job. That the board did the job well is attested by the fact that these four majestic towers are still there more than a century later, each one easily identified by the same markings decided on in the early 1870s, and each a lonely sentinel of the North Carolina coast well into its second century of service to mariners.

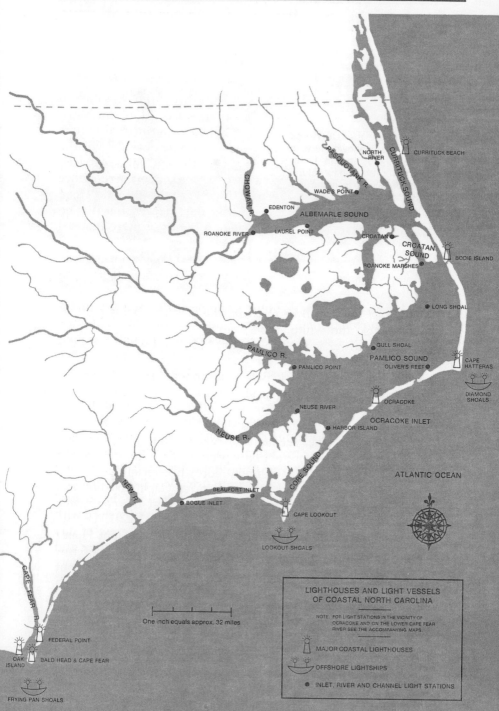

CURRITUCK BEACH

PASQUOTANK R.

NORTH RIVER

CURRITUCK SOUND

WADE'S POINT

CHOWAN R.

EDENTON

ALBEMARLE SOUND

ROANOKE RIVER

LAUREL POINT

CROATAN

CROATAN SOUND

BODIE ISLAND

ROANOKE MARSHES

LONG SHOAL

GULL SHOAL

PAMLICO R.

PAMLICO SOUND

CAPE HATTERAS

PAMLICO POINT

OLIVER'S REEF

DIAMOND SHOALS

NEUSE RIVER

OCRACOKE

OCRACOKE INLET

NEUSE R.

HARBOR ISLAND

CORE SOUND

ATLANTIC OCEAN

NEW R.

BEAUFORT INLET

BOGUE INLET

CAPE LOOKOUT

LOOKOUT SHOALS

CAPE FEAR R.

FEDERAL POINT

OAK ISLAND

BALD HEAD & CAPE FEAR

FRYING PAN SHOALS

One inch equals approx. 32 miles

LIGHTHOUSES AND LIGHT VESSELS
OF COASTAL NORTH CAROLINA

NOTE: FOR LIGHT STATIONS IN THE VICINITY OF
OCRACOKE AND ON THE LOWER CAPE FEAR
RIVER SEE THE ACCOMPANYING MAPS.

MAJOR COASTAL LIGHTHOUSES

OFFSHORE LIGHTSHIPS

INLET, RIVER AND CHANNEL LIGHT STATIONS

12

Conclusion

The days of hauling oil to the top of each lighthouse tower to provide fuel for the lamps have long since passed. All of the North Carolina lights are automated and equipped with timers that turn them on at dusk and off at dawn. Now a responsibility of the United States Coast Guard, they are checked and serviced periodically, for there is no longer a need to have keepers in residence at each of the light stations. Even at Cape Fear the old Bald Head light is still there, serving as a distinctive day marker, but it is no longer lighted, having been replaced in 1958 by a more modern lighthouse across the river mouth at Oak Island.

Yet even in the twentieth century modernization has not come all at once. Two temporary skeleton steel towers were erected briefly at Cape Fear and Cape Hatteras. The first, at Cape Fear, temporarily replaced Bald Head in 1903, but it has long since been destroyed. The second, erected in 1936, replaced the Cape Hatteras lighthouse temporarily. Both steel towers were located on wooded sandhills well back from the beach where erosion was less threatening. When the Cape Hatteras lighthouse was relighted in 1950, the second steel tower was also abandoned.

The very thought of lighthouses on the part of North Carolinians is apt to carry a feeling of solidity and permanence, and with justification. For today's visitors to the coastal lighthouses will see at Bald Head and Ocracoke the very same structures erected there in the early part of the last century. At isolated Cape Lookout they can easily conjure up visions of Confederate defenders hastily dismantling the lantern even as Federal forces approached up Shackleford Banks. At Cape Hatteras the majestic structure can be viewed with awe and wonder as to how Dexter Stetson and his crew of day laborers could possibly have done their job so well at that place and at that time. And at Bodie Island and Currituck Beach few visitors could fail to speculate as to how life was for the keepers and their families at those barren coastal outposts.

Those major coastal lights, however, are the sole survivors of the extensive network of aids to mariners placed in North Carolina waters by the old Light House Board. Throughout the interior waters the screw-piles are all gone, replaced for the most part by a series of smaller though more powerful automated beacons

A light perched atop a skeleton steel tower guarded the Cape Fear River as early as 1903, but it has long since been destroyed. (Photo from the files of the U.S. Coast Guard.)

mounted on poles or pyramid-shaped skeleton towers; functional, yes, but totally lacking in glamor and beauty and those distinctive features of which nostalgia is bred.

In truth the history of North Carolina's lighthouses during the past century has been for the most part dull and uninspiring, partly because the Light House Board did its job so well, and partly because the emphasis on the part of its successors has been on functional qualities rather than aesthetics, and probably rightly so. Whereas the fifth auditor in the eleven-year period between 1825 and 1836 placed nine light vessels on North Carolina stations, and the Light House Board replaced seven of those floating lights with screw-pile lighthouses during a period of just three years after the Civil War, the last century has seen just one major lighthouse construction project in North Carolina. Only offshore, beyond the shoals stretching out from the state's three dangerous capes, have there been concentrated efforts to provide better aids to navigation, and at only one, Frying Pan Shoals off Cape Fear, have those efforts provided fairly continuous and adequate warnings throughout the century.

The priority given the Frying Pan Shoals light is attributable in part at least to three factors. First, the Cape Fear River was and con-

In 1966 a light tower replaced the lightship at Frying Pan Shoals that had been in service since 1930. The new tower's steel legs are spread sixty feet apart and encased in steel pilings thirty-six inches in diameter, which in turn are driven 293 feet below the ocean floor. From its elevation of 130 feet, the tower's light is visible to mariners from seventeen miles. (Photo from the files of the U.S. Coast Guard.)

tinues to be North Carolina's major port. Second, the Cape Fear area is not as exposed as Cape Hatteras, not as close to the Gulf Stream nor as affected by the littoral drift, so that it is somewhat easier to maintain a lightship there. Finally, when storms approach or the lightship parts its moorings, it is only a short distance to safe anchorage in the Cape Fear River.

The first Frying Pan Shoals lightship was placed on station in 1854 and remained until it was removed at the outbreak of the Civil War. As soon as Federal forces secured Fort Fisher and gained control of the Cape Fear River, plans were made to put a lightship back on the station, and in late 1865 a two-masted schooner-rigged vessel was anchored off the tip of the shoals in ten fathoms of water. With its hull and the lower part of its masts painted yellow, and the words "Frying Pan Shoals" in bold black letters on each side, the vessel exhibited two lights at an elevation of forty feet above sea level.

For the next 101 years this vessel and its successors guarded the entrance to the Cape Fear River, leaving the station only temporarily for repairs or as the result of storm action. In 1966 the last of the Frying Pan Shoals lightships was removed, and a modern new Texas-tower type of structure replaced it.

Lookout Shoals, approximately midway between Cape Fear and Cape Hatteras, was considered as the site for an offshore lighthouse as early as 1806, but the idea was abandoned as impractical. For the

The Diamond Shoals light tower
replaced the Diamond lightship in
1967. Standing in fifty-four feet of
water, the light tower is visible from
a range of seventeen miles. (Photo
from the files of the U.S. Coast
Guard.)

next century there always seemed to be more urgent needs than
those at Lookout Shoals, and nothing was done to provide
navigational aids at the site other than occasional experiments with
different types of anchored buoys. Finally, in 1903 an old lightship
was placed at Lookout Shoals and plans were made to build a new
620-ton "first class steel steam light-vessel, with steam fog signal" for
the station.

On several occasions during the years that followed the Lookout
Shoals lightship was driven from its station in stormy weather, but
only for brief periods. Three of the crew members were drowned on
July 25, 1913, when their whaleboat was inadvertently run down by
the steamer *City of Atlanta*, to which they were attempting to transfer
mail from the lightship.

Finally, in 1933 the last of the Lookout Shoals lightships was
removed, to be replaced by unmanned buoys and other types of
relatively minor navigational aids.

The saga of Diamond Shoals remains singular, however, a continuing story of frustration and inadequacy that began with the
short-lived attempt to station a lightship there in the 1820s. In the
antebellum period almost every conceivable type of warning device
was considered for Diamond Shoals, and experiments were actually
carried out with many of them. First there were buoys of different
shapes and designs; then a whistling buoy—but someone stole the
whistle; and finally a bell boat, an unmanned vessel that was

anchored on the site in 1852 but four months later broke loose in a storm and was never seen or heard again.

So many vessels were shipwrecked in the vicinity of Diamond Shoals that it became known as the Graveyard of the Atlantic, and the complaints of mariners and insurance underwriters were at last acknowledged by the Light House Board when it ordered a survey as to the feasibility of placing a lightship there again. Instead of the lightship, however, the board decided to build a lighthouse on the outer fringes of the shoals, a project of such magnitude that Congress authorized an expenditure of up to half a million dollars for the purpose.

Engineers were convinced that advances in technology made the project feasible. The key was to be able to sink onto the shoals a huge circular watertight structure that could be pumped out while the work progressed. They designed a giant caisson, fifty-four feet in diameter and forty-five feet high, which was built in Norfolk and towed to the site in the summer of 1891. On July 1 the giant caisson was gently lowered to the bottom in a depth of between twenty-two and twenty-five feet of water, which left the sides still extended some twenty feet into the air. Almost immediately, however, the massive structure began to tilt as sand was washed away from the base by underwater currents; but even as efforts were being made to correct this problem a violent summer storm struck the area. When workmen returned to the site they found that the top of the caisson had been destroyed and much of the construction machinery lost, thus ending the first serious attempt to build a permanent lighthouse on Diamond Shoals.

Three years later yet another lighthouse proposal was made for Diamond Shoals, with the idea this time to sink heavy iron piles as the support for a skeleton tower. But in 1896 this plan was abandoned, and Congress appropriated funds for a lightship, which took up its station off the tip of the shoals on September 30, 1897. The Light House Board was satisfied with the performance of the Diamond Shoals lightship and reported that "with the improved means of mooring a lightship, she can be depended on with reasonable certainty to be on her station at all times." Congress nonetheless was pressured to authorize a private firm, headed by Albert E. Eells of Boston, to erect a Diamond Shoals lighthouse entirely at the firm's expense. An agreement was reached whereby the Eells group would receive payment of $750,000 if the proposed lighthouse survived a four-year trial operation, but the project never materialized.

For the next half century the Diamond Shoals lightship was a more or less permanent fixture at the lonely post off Cape Hatteras. In 1899 the original vessel, designated *Diamond Shoals Lightship Number 69*, was driven ashore near the cape; on several other occasions its successors were rammed by passing ships; and on August 6, 1918, the lightship guarding Diamond Shoals was sunk by a German submarine.

A replacement vessel soon took up the duty, and from then until the late 1960s Diamond Shoals remained "one of the most exposed stations for such a vessel in the world." Finally, in 1967 a modern elevated structure of Texas-tower design was constructed on the Outer Diamond, at long last relieving the tedium and turbulence for the crewmen on board the lightships that had been stationed there.

The future of North Carolina's lighthouses is as uncertain now as at any time in history. Most vessels, even the smaller fishing trawlers, are equipped with modern navigational aids. Electronic instruments such as loran make it possible for a captain to know almost exactly where he is at any time of day or night. The massive tower at Cape Hatteras has long been threatened by erosion, and recently the National Park Service has estimated that erosion will claim the old Cape Lookout lighthouse within a few years unless the migration of a nearby inlet is changed.

Maybe it will not matter then. Maybe lighthouses are no longer needed. But if the time comes when the century-old towers at Cape Hatteras and Cape Lookout, and at Bodie Island and Currituck Beach are abandoned; and if the even older structures at Bald Head and Ocracoke are declared surplus, it will mark the end of a glorious period of history on the North Carolina coast.

A Note on Research Sources

It is necessary to go to United States government records for most of the basic material on North Carolina lighthouses, and anyone undertaking serious research on the subject must inevitably delve into Record Group 26 at the National Archives in Washington, D.C. There the researcher will find extensive manuscript material in the form of ledgers, journals, correspondence files, and a wide variety of other related papers. Some of it is consolidated in folders dealing with specific light stations, but most is arranged chronologically for lighthouse districts or for the entire lighthouse establishment. Especially helpful are the clipping files on individual lighthouses—part printed and part manuscript material—and the printed annual light lists, the latter being available also in other selected libraries and repositories.

Two printed volumes in my library have been referred to over and over again as the research and writing progressed. One, 255 pages including an index, is entitled *Laws of the United States relating to the establishment, support, and management of the light-houses, light-vessels, monuments, beacons, spindles, buoys, and public piers of the United States, from August 7, 1789 to March 3, 1855*, compiled by order of the Light House Board and published in Washington in 1855. The other, running to 1,060 pages with a good index, is *Compilation of Public Documents and extracts from reports and papers relating to light-houses, light-vessels, and illuminating apparatus, and to beacons, buoys and fog signals, 1789 to 1871*. This was prepared by the United States Light House Establishment and published by the Government Printing Office in Washington in 1871.

Helpful also have been various volumes of the Congressional Serial Set, sometimes known as the Government Serial Publications. Though these are available in some libraries, they are difficult to use since the complete set runs to more than 2,000 volumes. The annual reports of the Light House Board, and later of the commissioner of lighthouses, sometimes contain detailed information not available elsewhere.

Anyone contemplating extensive research on the subject of North Carolina lighthouses would do well to make contact with the office of the historian of the United States Coast Guard. The Coast Guard currently has custody of lighthouses, and Dr. Robert

Scheina, the present historian, provided me with much time-saving guidance and assistance in this undertaking.

For the period before the federal government assumed responsibility for lighthouses in 1789, a primary source is the twenty-six volume *Colonial and State Records of North Carolina*, edited by William L. Saunders and Walter Clark, with four volumes of index by Stephen B. Weeks. Colonial North Carolina newspapers contain some material, as do the deed books and other records in the coastal counties.

The Mariners' Museum at Newport News, Virginia, has an extensive collection of lighthouse materials, including artifacts and models that provide a unique opportunity for visual research.

A number of nongovernment printed publications were checked, but only one proved of significant value. This is Francis Ross Holland, Jr.'s, *America's Lighthouses: Their Illustrated History since 1716*, a profusely illustrated volume of 226 pages plus index, published in 1972 by the Stephen Greene Press, Brattleboro, Vermont. Holland, a historian with the National Park Service, has also prepared detailed reports on the lighthouses located within the Park Service facilities on the Outer Banks and has been most gracious in providing guidance as this work was undertaken.

Index

A

Albemarle Sound, 8, 30, 31, 53, 61
Alexandria, Egypt: site of first recorded lighthouse, 2
Americans: build first lighthouse at Boston, 4. *See also* United States
America's Lighthouses, 49, 58
Argand, Ami: invents lighting system, 49
Ashby's Harbor, 56

B

Bald Head Island, 37-38, 56; lighthouse of, pictured, 13, 36; site of first North Carolina lighthouse, 11-17
Bald Head lighthouse, 57, 71, 76; and complaints of its inadequacy, 22; pictured, 13, 36
Barron, James: designs Diamond Shoals lightship, 27
Bartlett, Robbins & Co., 64
Bath, N.C., 8, 16; and need for pilots, 9; port of, to levy duty for lighthouse construction, 13
Beacon: defined, 37
Beacon Island, 46, 53, 55
Beattie, Dawson & Co., 64
Beaufort, N.C., 7, 21; port of, to levy duty for lighthouse construction, 13
Beaufort Inlet, 47, 56. *See also* Old Topsail Inlet
Blackbeard, 9
Blount, John Gray: makes Shell Castle Island a major shipping center, 15-17
Blunt's Coast Pilot, 23
Bodie Island, 71; and confusion with Pea Island, 42; second lighthouse for, 51
Bodie Island lighthouse, 53, 76; destroyed by Confederate forces, 55; destroyed during Civil War, 63; establishment of, 42-44; pat-terned after Cape Lookout lighthouse, 67-68; pictured, 67, 68; to be painted with horizontal bands, 69
Bogue Banks, 47, 56
Bogue Inlet, 5, 47
Bogue Sound, 5
Bonnet, Stede, 9
Boston, Mass.: site of first lighthouse in America, 4
Brant Island Shoal, 31, 57, 60
Britain: lighthouse establishment of, considered better than United States', 45
British: land at Ocracoke Island during War of 1812, 23. *See also* English
Brunswick Town, N.C., 35
Burnside, Ambrose E.: leads Union attack on Roanoke Island, 55-56

C

Calabash, N.C., 5
Campbell: revenue cutter commanded by Napoleon Coste, 42
Campbell's Island, 37, 38, 57
Cape Fear, 7, 21, 24, 25, 46, 71, 72, 73
Cape Fear River, 8, 21, 73; and congressional appropriations for navigational aids, 36-37; and picture of skeleton steel tower, 72; and screw-pile lighthouses of, 61; becomes lifeline of Confederacy, 56-57; efforts to provide lighthouse at mouth of, 11-17; North Carolina's single deepwater channel, 7, 35
Cape Hatteras, 5, 7, 24, 25, 42, 47, 71, 73, 76; and unique problems of marking it, 48; lighthouse of, built, 18-21; lighthouse of, pictured, 20
Cape Hatteras lighthouse: and construction of new one, 63-66; and destruction of old tower, 66-67;

pictured, 62, 65, 68; receives first-order Fresnel lens, 49; rendered inoperative by Confederate forces, 55; termed a "disgrace," 48; to be painted in spiral bands, 68. *See also* Diamond Shoals

Cape Henry, 63, 68

Cape Lookout, 5, 7, 24, 25, 71; lighthouse for, constructed, 21-22

Cape Lookout lighthouse, 56; becomes model for later lighthouses, 51-52; pictured, 50, 51, 68; threatened by erosion, 76; to be painted with checkers, 69; used as model for new Cape Hatteras lighthouse, 63

Cat Island, Bahamas, 19

Cedar Island, 31

Charleston, S.C., 4

Chesapeake Bay, 14, 42, 63

Chicamacomico, N.C., 43, 55

City of Atlanta: inadvertently runs down lightship crew, 74

Civil War, 73; and impact on navigational aids, 53-57

Colombo, Antonio: tends Genoa light, 2

Columbus, Christopher: uncle of, tends Genoa light, 2

Commerce: of North Carolina, affected by shallow waters, 7, 8, 9

Confederacy: attempts to fortify Outer Banks, 53, 55; depends on Cape Fear River lifeline, 56-57

Confederate forces: blow up Bodie Island lighthouse, 55; destroy lower Cape Fear lights, 57; render Cape Lookout lighthouse inoperative, 56

Congress, U.S.: and first lighthouses built in North Carolina, 24; appropriates funds for Bodie Island lighthouse, 43; appropriates funds for Cape Hatteras lighthouse, 63; appropriates funds for lighthouse at Ocracoke Island, 23; appropriates funds for lightship at Diamond Shoals, 75; appropriates funds for navigational aids on Cape Fear River, 36-37; appropriates funds for new lighthouse at Bodie Island, 51; assumes responsibility for building lighthouses, 13-17; authorizes funds for light vessel at Diamond Shoals, 25; blamed for inferior lighthouse establishment, 45; considers placing lighthouses on shoals, 25; delays appropriations for Cape Hatteras light, 21; organizes Light House Board, 46; passes act for Cape Hatteras light, 18; sets pay scale for lightship crew, 27

Cordouan: site of French light, 2

Core Sound, 30, 31

Corolla, N.C., 68

Coste, Napoleon L.: recommends lighthouses for Outer Banks, 42, 43

Croatan Sound, 30, 31, 53, 55, 57, 60

Crossman, George J.: installs flashing lens at Cape Hatteras lighthouse, 66

Currituck: port of, to levy duty for lighthouse construction, 13

Currituck Beach, 71

Currituck Beach lighthouse, 68, 76; pictured, 69; to retain its natural red brick color, 69

Currituck Sound, 5, 61

D

Dearborn, Henry: contractor for Cape Hatteras light, 21

Decatur, Stephen, 27

Delaware, 5

Delaware Bay, 7

Diamond Shoals, 19, 48; and attempts to mark it safely, 74-76; as crucial location for navigational aid, 25; light tower of, pictured, 74. *See also* Cape Hatteras

Diamond Shoals lightship, 42; pictured, 26; problems of, 27-29

Diamond Shoals Lightship 69: driven ashore in storm, 76; pictured, 26

E

Eckford, Henry: builds light vessel for Diamond Shoals, 27
Eddystone light: built by English in 1698, 3
Edenton, N.C., 8, 16, 50; and need for pilots, 9
Edenton Bay, 61
Eells, Albert E.: pressures Congress to erect lighthouse at Diamond Shoals, 75
Egyptians: build first lighthouse at Pharos, 2
Elizabeth City, N.C., 50
Elliott, Jesse: clashes with Captain Erickson about Diamond Shoals lightship, 27
English: and early settlement of North Carolina, 1; build lighthouses, 2, 3. *See also* British
Erickson, Christian: commands Diamond Shoals lightship, 27-28
Etheridge, John B.: appointed keeper of Bodie Island lighthouse, 44; sells site for Bodie Island lighthouse, 67

F

Federal Point, 60, 61; beacon, 23; lighthouse, 57
Foix, Louis de: designs massive light for French, 2
Fort Clark, 53, 55
Fort Fisher: battles of, 56-57; falls to Union forces, 73
Fort Hatteras, 53, 55
Fort Macon, 47, 56
Fort Ocracoke, 53, 55
Fort Oregon, 53, 55
France: and development of lighting system, 49; lighthouse establishment of, considered better than United States', 45
French: build lighthouses, 2

Fresnel, Augustin: invents lens for lighthouses, 49
Fresnel lens: installed at Bodie Island lighthouse, 51; installed at Cape Lookout lighthouse, 52; ordered for all American lighthouses, 58
Frying Pan Shoals, 7, 14; and efforts to mark effectively, 72-73; light tower of, pictured, 73; marked with lightship, 46
Fulford, Joseph: deeds site for Cape Lookout light, 21

G

Gallatin, Albert, 22
Gaskill, Jacob: owns site of Ocracoke lighthouse, 24
General Assembly, N.C.: depends on pilots to mark shoals, 9; finalizes transfer of land to federal government for Cape Hatteras light, 20; levies tax to construct lighthouse at Bald Head, 11; passes act for construction of lighthouse at Ocracoke Inlet, 12; transfers lighthouse sites to federal government, 14
Genoa: site of twelfth-century lighthouse, 2
Georgia, 5
Germans: build lighthouses, 2
Gibbons, Francis A.: builds Bodie Island lighthouse, 43
Granganimo (Indian), 1
Graveyard of the Atlantic: surrounds Diamond Shoals, 75
Gulf Stream, 48, 73; collides with Labrador Current off Cape Hatteras, 19
Gull Shoal, 61

H

Hamilton, Alexander, 15
Harbor Island, 60; screw-pile lighthouse of, pictured, 59
Harbor Island Bar, 31
Hatteras Inlet, 53, 55, 57, 60

Hatteras Island, 42, 55
Holden, Lief: assumes command of Diamond Shoals lightship, 28-29
Holland, Francis Ross, Jr.: describes screw-pile lighthouses, 58; explains Fresnel lens, 49
Horseshoe Shoal, 37, 40, 57, 60
Howard, William, Jr.: provides land for Ocracoke light, 13
Hurricane: creates Oregon and Hatteras inlets in 1846, 43

I

Ida Nicholson: sinks while transporting materials for Cape Hatteras lighthouse, 65
Indians: learn to identify landmarks for navigating, 1; pictured with canoes, 3
Inlets: formation of, explained, 22; shifting of, causes confusion on Outer Banks, 43
Isaacs, Joseph: map by, 54
Italians: take lead in lighthouse construction, 2

J

J. Parker: goes ashore while transporting materials for Cape Hatteras lighthouse, 65
Jacksonville, Fla., 18
Jennett, Aquilla: owns site of Cape Hatteras light, 20
Jennett, Christian: guardian to owners of Cape Hatteras site for lighthouse, 20
Jennett, Jabez: owns site of Cape Hatteras light, 20
Jennett, Mary: owns site of Cape Hatteras light, 20
Jennett, William: owns site of Cape Hatteras light, 20

K

Key West, Fla., 19
Kinnakeet, N.C., 19, 55
Kitty Hawk, N.C., 42, 63

L

Labrador Current: collides with Gulf Stream off Cape Hatteras, 19
Lamps. *See* Lighting
Laurel Point, 61
Lennox and Burgess Co., 64
Lens. *See* Fresnel lens; Lighting
Lewis, Winslow: develops lighting system, 49; installs lantern at Bodie Island lighthouse, 43
Light House Board, 71; and efforts to mark Diamond Shoals, 75; decrees distinctive markings for lighthouses, 68-69; determines to elevate Cape Hatteras lighthouse, 48; does job well, 72; emphasizes need for new lighthouse at Cape Hatteras, 63; hires own crew to build Cape Hatteras lighthouse, 64; installs Fresnel lens at Cape Lookout lighthouse, 52; organized, 44-47; orders first-order lens for Cape Hatteras lighthouse, 66; orders installation of Fresnel lens at Cape Hatteras lighthouse, 49; orders lighthouses for North Carolina interior waters, 51; replaces light vessels with screw-pile lighthouses, 58
Light vessels: common characteristics of, 30; defined, 25; difficult life aboard, described, 28-29; in North Carolina interior waters, 30-33, 36; placed at Diamond Shoals, 75-76; placed at Frying Pan Shoals, 73; placed at Lookout Shoals, 74
Lightboats. *See* Light vessels
Lighters: devised for estuarine waters, 8; used to transport materials for building of Cape Hatteras lighthouse, 64, 65
Lighthouses: along southern coast deemed useless, 45-46; and development of screw-piles, 58; and lighting systems, 49; and logistics for building at Cape Hatteras, 64; and technology for building at

Cape Hatteras, 65-66; as light vessels, 25; defined, 37; first in North Carolina, 11-17; first recorded instances of, 2; to be re-organized by federal government, 44-46. *See also* Congress, U.S.; Light House Board; Light vessels; Pleasanton, Stephen; Screw-pile lighthouses; Treasury, U.S.

Lighting: and flashing lens for Cape Hatteras lighthouse, 66; appara-tus for, at Bodie Island, 44; ap-paratus for, in United States term-ed "obsolete," 45; systems of, in lighthouses, 49

Lightships. *See* Light vessels

Lindsey, Edmund C.: sells site of Currituck Beach lighthouse, 68

Long Shoal, 30, 31, 32, 60

Lookout Shoals: and efforts to mark it safely, 73-74

Louisiana, 5

Lyon, Lucius, 32

M

Maps: by James Wimble (1733), 8; by John White (1585), 6; of Cape Fear River lights, 34; of North Carolina lighthouses, 70; of pre-Civil War North Carolina light-houses, *frontispiece*; of seat of war at Hatteras Inlet, 54

Marsh Point, 31

Martin, Alexander: transmits gift of land for Ocracoke light, 13

Martin, Josiah: petitioned by white pilots, 9

Maryland, 5

Meloria: site of lighthouse in 1157, 2

Midgett, John: deeds land for Bodie Island lighthouse, 43

Mitchell, Alexander: invents screw-pile lighthouses, 58

N

Nags Head, N.C., 42, 65

National Park Service: warns of ero-sion at Cape Lookout lighthouse, 76

Negroes: serve as pilots, 9

Neuse River, 30, 31, 60

New Bern, N.C., 8, 16, 31; and need for pilots, 9

New Inlet, 37, 40, 56, 61; renders Bald Head light useless, 22-23

New Jersey, 5

New York, 5

Nine Feet Shoal, 31, 32

Norfolk, Va., 25, 28, 29, 75

North Carolina: and lighthouses in-stalled under Stephen Pleasanton, 42; and the future of its light-houses, 76; benefits from Light House Board, 46-47; coast of, characterized, 5-10, 18; commerce of, affected by shallow waters, 7, 8, 9; interior waters of, marked with lightboats, 29-33; lighthouses of, in past century, 72; rivers of, described, 35; state government of, begins lighthouse construction, 11; strategic importance of, in Civil War, 53

North River, 60, 61

Northwest Point, 57, 60

O

Oak Island, 37, 38, 61, 71; rear beacon of, pictured, 39

Ocracoke, N.C., 21, 71; and efforts to provide lighthouse for, 11-17

Ocracoke Inlet, 24, 30, 31, 36, 46, 53; and activities of pilots, 9-10

Ocracoke Island: and community of pilots, 10

Ocracoke lighthouse, 42, 57, 76; con-struction of, 23-24; pictured, 24

Old Rock. *See* Shell Castle Island

Old Topsail Inlet, 8, 21; provides access to Beaufort, 7. *See also* Beaufort Inlet

Oliver's Reef, 60

Oregon Inlet, 51, 53, 55, 67; cuts through Bodie Island in 1846, 43

Orton's Point, 37, 38, 57
Outer Banks, 5; and defense of Confederacy, 53; and need for lighthouses equally spaced, 63; and recommendations for lighthouses, 42

P

Pamlico Point, 57
Pamlico River, 30, 31
Pamlico Sound, 5, 8, 15, 30, 31, 53, 61
Pamtico Point, 31
Pamtico Sound, 30
Pasquotank River, 30, 32, 51
Paul Gamiel's Hill, 63
Pea Island, 63; and confusion with Bodie Island, 42
Pennsylvania, 7
Pharos of Alexandria: engraving of, *facing p. 1*; first recorded lighthouse, 2
Philadelphia, Pa., 7
Phoenicians: build ancient lighthouse, 2
Pigott, Elijah: deeds site for Cape Lookout light, 21
Pilot Town: on Ocracoke Island, 10
Pilots: essential to coastal navigation, 9-11; navigate Cape Fear River, 35; protest activities of Negroes, 9
Pirates, 9
Pleasanton, Stephen: and program for lightboats in interior waters, 29-33, 35-36; establishes Bodie Island lighthouse, 42; orders repair of Diamond Shoals lightship, 29; oversees nation's lighthouses, 25; reign of, ends, 44; removes Captain Erickson from command of Diamond Shoals lightship, 27-28
Porter, Noah: builds Ocracoke lighthouse, 24
Portland Head, Me., 14
Portsmouth, N.C.: as bustling maritime center, 15
Price's Creek, 37, 39-40, 57

Price's Creek lighthouse: pictured, 40, 41
Privateers, 3, 9; of British, harass shipping, 23

R

Raleigh, Sir Walter, 1
Reflectors. *See* Fresnel lens; Lighting
Revolutionary War: leaves navigational hazards in Cape Fear River, 35
Roanoke: port of, to levy duty for lighthouse construction, 13
Roanoke Island, 1, 31, 53, 55; battle of, 55-56
Roanoke Marshes, 31, 32, 50, 55, 57, 60; screw-pile lighthouse of, pictured, 60
Roanoke River, 60
Rock of Gibraltar, 1
Romans: build thirty lighthouses in empire, 2
Royal Shoal, 15, 31, 57, 60

S

Savannah, Ga., 4
Screw-pile lighthouses, 51, 71-72; description of, 58-60; life aboard, characterized, 58-59
Shell Castle Island: site of beacon for Ocracoke Inlet, 15-17, 21
Shell Castle lighthouse: and complaints on its inadequacy, 22; becomes useless, 23; pictured, 16
Shoals: afflict North Carolina waterways, 5-7; are inadequately marked before the American Revolution, 9-10; stretch seaward from North Carolina capes, 25. *See also* North Carolina, interior waters of; Screw-pile lighthouses
Shubrick, W. B.: chairs board investigating nation's lighthouses, 44
Smith, Benjamin: offers site for first North Carolina lighthouse, 11
Smith, Nicholas M.: furnishes bricks for Cape Hatteras lighthouse, 64

Smith's Island. *See* Bald Head Island
South Carolina, 5
Southport, N.C., 35, 38, 39
Southwest Point of Royal Shoal, 31, 60
Spain: site of ancient lighthouse, 2
Starke, L. D.: recommends lighthouse for Roanoke Marshes, 50
Stetson, Dexter, 71; builds Bodie Island lighthouse, 67; directs construction of Cape Hatteras lighthouse, 64-66

T

Tatham, William: describes Cape Hatteras light as eyesore, 21; inspects Cape Lookout for site of lighthouse, 22
Technology: to build Cape Hatteras lighthouse, 65-66; to place permanent lighthouse at Diamond Shoals, 75
Texas tower: replaces lightships, 73, 76
Tilles, Samuel: appointed keeper of Bodie Island lighthouse, 43
Tower of Hercules: stands in Spain, 2
Treasury, U.S.: responsibility of, for lighthouses, 25; secretary of, approves light vessel for Ocracoke Inlet, 23; secretary of, instructed to investigate lighthouse establishment, 44; secretary of, to erect lighthouse at Cape Hatteras, 18
Turks: build lighthouse, 2

U

Union forces: encampment of, around Cape Hatteras lighthouse, pictured, 20; repair lights, 57; seize control of Fort Fisher, 57; seize Forts Hatteras and Clark, 55; take control of Albemarle region, 55-56
United States: inferior lighthouse establishment of, criticized, 45. *See also* Americans; Congress, U.S.; Treasury, U.S.

United States Coast Guard: assumes responsibility for lighthouses, 71
Upper Jettee, 37, 40-41, 57

V

Van Pelt: heirs of, claim lighthouse property, 32
Virginia, 5, 63
Virginia Beach, Va., 42

W

Wade's Point, 31, 51, 57, 60
Wallace, John: death of, 23; makes Shell Castle Island a major shipping center, 15-17
Wanchese, N.C., 31
War of 1812: and effect on Ocracoke shipping, 23
Washington, N.C., 31
Western Bar, 37
White, John: 1585 map by, 6; paintings of, 3
Williams, John: provides land for Ocracoke light, 13
Williams, Joseph: provides land for Ocracoke light, 13
Williams, William: provides land for Ocracoke light, 13
Willoughby Spit: site of first American light vessel, 25
Wilmington, N.C., 38, 40, 41, 56, 61; merchants of, appeal for navigational aids, 36; replaces Brunswick Town as major trading center, 35
Wimble, James: 1733 map by, 8
Wingina (Indian), 1
Withers, Thomas: furnishes bricks for Bald Head light, 12